Cambridge Elements ☰

Elements in Shakespeare Performance
edited by
W. B. Worthen
Barnard College

EXTENDED REALITY SHAKESPEARE

Aneta Mancewicz
Royal Holloway, University of London

CAMBRIDGE
UNIVERSITY PRESS

CAMBRIDGE
UNIVERSITY PRESS

Shaftesbury Road, Cambridge CB2 8EA, United Kingdom

One Liberty Plaza, 20th Floor, New York, NY 10006, USA

477 Williamstown Road, Port Melbourne, VIC 3207, Australia

314–321, 3rd Floor, Plot 3, Splendor Forum, Jasola District Centre,
New Delhi – 110025, India

103 Penang Road, #05–06/07, Visioncrest Commercial, Singapore 238467

Cambridge University Press is part of Cambridge University Press & Assessment,
a department of the University of Cambridge.

We share the University's mission to contribute to society through the pursuit of
education, learning and research at the highest international levels of excellence.

www.cambridge.org
Information on this title: www.cambridge.org/9781009044561

DOI: 10.1017/9781009043854

First published 2024

A catalogue record for this publication is available from the British Library.

ISBN 978-1-009-04456-1 Paperback
ISSN 2516-0117 (online)
ISSN 2516-0109 (print)

Additional resources for this publication at http://www.cambridge.org/Mancewicz

Extended Reality Shakespeare

Elements in Shakespeare Performance

DOI: 10.1017/9781009043854
First published online: February 2024

Aneta Mancewicz
Royal Holloway, University of London

Author for correspondence: Aneta Mancewicz, aneta.mancewicz@rhul.ac.uk

ABSTRACT: This Element argues for the importance of extended reality as an innovative force that changes our understanding of theatre and Shakespeare. It shows how including augmented and virtual realities in performance can reconfigure the senses of the experiencers, enabling them to actively engage with technology. Such engagements can, in turn, result in new forms of presence, embodiment, eventfulness, and interaction. In drawing on Shakespeare's dramas as source material, the Element recognises the growing practice of staging them in an extended reality mode and their potential to advance the development of extended reality. Given Shakespeare's emphasis on metatheatre, his works can inspire the layering of environments as well as the experiences of transition between those environments – both features that distinguish extended reality. An examination of selected works in this Element unveils creative convergences between Shakespeare's dramaturgy and digital technology.

KEYWORDS: Shakespeare, extended reality (XR), digital performance, virtual reality (VR), augmented reality (AR)

ISBNs: 9781009044561 (PB), 9781009043854 (OC)
ISSNs: 2516-0117 (online), 2516-0109 (print)

Contents

Introduction

I am scanning my living room with an iPhone. The screen shows an avatar of Gonzalo, a courtier from Shakespeare's *The Tempest*, delivering a utopian vision of society. He begins with a problem: 'Had I plantation of this isle, my lord, And were the king on't, what would I do?' (Shakespeare, 1999: 2.1.144). He finishes with a proposal: 'nature should bring forth/ Of its own kind all foison, all abundance/ To feed my innocent people' (Shakespeare, 1999, 2.1.165). The speech is performed in real time by an actor (Tonderai Munyevu) who is present in a remote studio, while we as the audience are watching the performance on personal devices at homes. Moving around, we can see the avatar very closely and from different perspectives. We can also assist him in bringing his plan to fruition. We do this by tapping the screen to plant seeds, which will grow into fabulous foliage and take over the interiors of our living rooms (Figure 1 and Video 1).

As an instance of extended reality, Gonzalo's green dream is both elaborate and ephemeral. It examines the possibility of humans living in harmony with nature, but it also explores human co-habitation with technology. While we are transforming the image of our personal space by introducing virtual vegetation, we can experience a hybrid kind of reality. In this moment, we have to combine the tactile stimuli of being in a physical environment with the visual stimuli of having the same space mediated and transformed on the screen. As virtual elements are changing our perception of the physical space by affecting our sense of size and scale, Gonzalo's utopia turns into an exploration of the environment that is at once palimpsestic and playful. Placed at the centre of this exploration, we intently and intensely attend to our proprioception. We are present.

The scene described just now is at the centre of Nexus Studios' *The Tempest* (2020), an augmented reality performance designed to take place in the users' homes. I introduce it as an example of an extended reality Shakespeare production in the first extensive study on this topic. 'Extended reality' (commonly abbreviated to XR) is an umbrella term that currently covers augmented, virtual, and mixed reality (respectively abbreviated to AR, VR, and MR), but might come to include future technologies as well (Çöltekin et al., 2020: 2; Dalton, 2021: 2, 5–6; Rauschnabel et al., 2022: 12).

Figure 1 *The Tempest* (2020). Courtesy of Nexus Studios.

As Arzu Çöltekin et al. (2020: 2) note, the term captures different degrees of physical and virtual environments, and in this sense it is akin to the continuum from reality to virtuality proposed by Milgram et al. (1994: 283) under the label of 'mixed reality'. Indeed, the terms 'extended reality' and 'mixed reality' are often used synonymously, and I will follow this usage in this Element. The term 'extended reality', however, has gained dominance among practitioners and professionals in recent years, becoming 'the industry's new favorite buzz word' (Goode, 2019). It is also quickly gaining traction in academia. For these reasons, I tend to favour the term 'extended reality' over 'mixed reality'. More specifically, I apply it to examine the transformative effects of augmented and virtual reality on the audience's perception of space, time, and the body in adaptations of Shakespeare's plays.

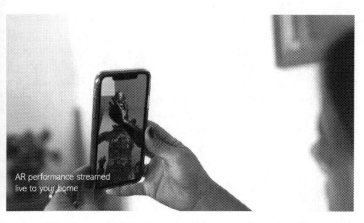

Video 1 *The Tempest* (2020). Courtesy of Nexus Studios. Video file available at http://www.cambridge.org/Mancewicz

This Element argues for the importance of extended reality as an innovative force that changes our understanding of theatre and Shakespeare. It shows how the possibility of experiencing different realities can reconfigure the senses of the experiencers, enabling them to actively engage with technology. This, in turn, results in new forms of presence, embodiment, eventfulness, and interaction. In drawing on Shakespeare's dramas as source material, the Element recognises the expanding tradition of staging them in an extended reality mode and their potential to advance the development of extended reality. Given Shakespeare's emphasis on metatheatre, his works can inspire the layering of environments as well as the experiences of transition between those environments – both features that distinguish extended reality. An examination of selected works in this Element unveils creative convergences between Shakespeare's dramaturgy and digital technology.

Extended reality is transforming theatre practice. It allows the participants to simultaneously experience material and digitally produced worlds, and in some cases also to activate virtual elements while remaining anchored in the physical setting. This changes the audience's perception of space, time, their own body, but also other bodies (those of performers and other participants) in unique ways. Applications of extended reality in performance rely on increasingly widespread technologies of augmented and virtual reality, which have an exciting and exceptional potential for novel forms of experience and engagement.

Some of the most discussed applications of extended reality in theatre have involved Shakespeare adaptations, for example Tender Claws' *Tempest* (2020), a live online performance in virtual reality, and the Royal Shakespeare Company's (RSC) *Dream* (2021), a live online performance with actors in a studio working with motion capture and virtual reality. Shakespeare's plays lend themselves particularly well to extended reality. They are richly imaginative, profoundly adaptable, and inherently metatheatrical. As such, they invite the layering of physical and virtual environments as different orders of representation; they also encourage moments of transition between these environments that inspire self-reflexivity. Historically, some of the most groundbreaking forms of staging have been trialled in Shakespeare's performances, which means that they offer particularly useful material for tracing the development of Western theatre. Following this tradition, this Element will discuss recent Shakespeare adaptations that have applied different strategies of merging physical and virtual worlds to redefine our understanding of performance, perception, and presence. The investigation of the selected productions will aim to identify ways in which Shakespeare's dramaturgical strategies might contribute to the development of extended reality in performance. Such an approach resonates with Jennifer Roberts-Smith's observation that '[n]ew technologies do not bring new affordances to Shakespeare; rather, "Shakespeare" (as that conceptual field has been understood and instantiated by artists, audiences, scholars, teachers, and students) will bring new opportunities for meaning-making to VR, just as it has to earlier technologies as they have emerged and have been configured in relation to one another' (Roberts-Smith, 2022: 4–5). In extended reality adaptations, Shakespeare's texts tend to serve as more than just readily available material for staging; instead, they function as an important inspiration for bold experiments with dramaturgy, imagery, characterisation, and audience engagement.

There are also other compelling reasons to turn to Shakespeare when examining extended reality. First of all, pioneering software and hardware tools have been frequently used in Shakespeare adaptations, so there is ample material for analysis and comparison. Addressing the popularity of Shakespeare's plays among practitioners experimenting with digital technologies, this Element makes it clear that this is not a coincidence as there are textual, theatrical, and cultural aspects of Shakespeare's work that invite combinations of physical and virtual environments. Second, there are already theoretical frameworks for discussing digital tools in and through Shakespeare, articulated in a number of publications that address technology in Shakespeare's theatre (Mancewicz, 2014; Cartelli, 2019; Aebischer, 2020; Worthen, 2020; Sullivan, 2022). Finally, Shakespeare's works hold extraordinary currency in terms of theatrical influence, cultural capital, and critical resonance. A spotlight on staging Shakespeare makes it possible to revisit and revise our assumptions about theatre as a medium but also about modes of representation and cultural participation.

Context

Previous scholarship (e.g., Benford and Giannachi, 2011; Weijdom, 2017) has recognised the crucial role of physical and virtual hybrids in transforming performance practice. It has investigated their impact on evolving patterns of production and reception, introducing invaluable theoretical tools and examining examples of practice. However, the field of theatre and performance studies still lacks a systematic approach and critical tools that might fully capture the implications of augmented and virtual reality for the evolution in stage practice, in particular their power to make us reconceive the essential characteristics of theatre and our categorisation of this medium. Addressing this lack is especially important given the latest technological advancements and the wave of innovative productions that have pushed the boundaries of performance even further.

At the same time, we still need a comprehensive account of extended reality applications in performances of Shakespeare. Recent publications on staging Shakespeare during the Covid-19 pandemic have been useful in examining artistic efforts to merge live and digital worlds (Aebischer, 2021; Allred et al., 2022), but they have focused on a broad range of formats, without addressing the specific opportunities and challenges of augmented and virtual reality technologies, which provide audience members with unique experiences of hybridity, embodiment, interactivity, and immersion. Meanwhile, the growing interest in Shakespeare and digital pedagogy has emphasised important links between Shakespeare and the virtual (e.g., Wittek and McInnis, 2022), but it has not fully explored their implications for performance practice.

To fill this gap, the Element focuses on augmented and virtual reality in staging Shakespeare. So far they have been extensively studied from the perspective of human–computer interactions, with relatively few contributions from performance studies. This Element applies an interdisciplinary methodology that brings together a number of fields, mainly human–computer interactions, performance studies, and Shakespeare studies. It also includes insights from two practice-as-research projects on which I worked as a researcher/dramaturg: augmented and virtual reality adaptations of *Hamlet* with the Brussels-based CREW collective (2016–21) and an augmented reality version of *The Tempest* with the animation and film studio Nexus Studios (2020).

In collecting extended reality adaptations for discussion and analysis, I have sought to feature culturally and geographically diverse examples to counter what Aswin Punathambekar and Sriram Mohan (2019: 4) denounce as 'universalizing tendencies of Anglo-American discourse' in the research on digital cultures. Amrita Sen notes how these 'universalizing tendencies' are especially visible in Shakespeare scholarship, where, despite the growing interest in the playwright's participation in the digital media culture, little attention is paid to digital Shakespeare practice in the Global South. She writes: 'What is often missing from these conversations . . . is how digital Shakespeares are created or experienced outside of Anglo-America, in spaces that often coincide with the post-colonies marked by unequal access to digital resources and complex histories of Shakespeare transmissions' (Sen, 2022: 3).

Despite my best efforts, however, I have not been able to locate extended reality theatre adaptations of Shakespeare from the Global South. Even though the examples range from professional productions to university research projects, the Element covers performance practice that has emerged from metropolitan centres in Europe and North America.

The absence might be owing to limited circulation of extended reality work. Given their novelty and technologically experimental status, augmented and virtual reality shows are often available only to a few users during a handful of showings in academic settings, and unless the work is distributed more widely through public presentations and publications, it might not be given much recognition and credit. The international success of the RSC's *Dream*, which – according to the company's tweet from 28 July 2021 – was watched in March 2021 by 65,000 people from 92 countries, is an exception. The RSC production owed its astounding popularity to its combining the high cultural profile of the Stratford-based company with an access requirement of relatively low-threshold technology. The contrast between *Dream*'s extraordinary dissemination and the modest reach of many other productions, together with their geographical concentration in the Global North, puts into perspective aspirational claims about the democratising potential of digital technologies.

At the same time, the higher concentration of extended reality theatre in the Anglo-American context exposes geopolitical disparity concerning the availability of specialised skill sets and tools, but also unequal opportunities in terms of public funding to support costly collaborative work that is required for the design of augmented and virtual reality. Several productions referenced in this Element were financed through the Audiences of the Future project, delivered by UK Research and Innovation, in which £39.3 million was invested in the development of virtual, augmented, and mixed reality technologies to enhance audience experience. Without this financial backing, many companies and research groups would not have been able to experiment and take risks. They would not have had the freedom to work on prototypes, free from the pressure of producing a polished product for the audience.

The access of audiences and artists to extended reality performances thus depends on a range of technological factors such as the affordability of devices, internet speed, and digital literacy. It also remains tied to economic, political, social, and cultural conditions. As Sen reminds us, '[t]o speak of the digital is to acknowledge a heterogeneous space with differing levels of technical competence, bandwidth, and participation' (Sen, 2022: 7). Once we recognise this heterogeneity as the crucial context for creation and participation in extended reality performances, we can become more aware of biases and restraints in the design, dissemination, and discussion of such work. While investigation of digital inequalities is not the subject of this Element, such inequalities form an essential, underlying basis for examining the theory and the practice of extended reality. Awareness of these inequalities is also necessary if we want to truly open up digital theatre practice to a diverse range of artists and audiences, so that the field can become not only more equitable but also more exciting.

Contribution

Drawing on a range of disciplines and methodologies, the Element provides a systematic and interdisciplinary investigation into how extended reality adaptations of Shakespeare incorporate three fundamental theatre concepts: space, time, and interactivity. By highlighting these concepts, extended reality is encouraging a review of our understanding of theatre itself. While previous studies have focused on defining extended reality in theatre, the objective of this Element is to reconsider theatre in the context of extended reality. As William Worthen observes, '[t]he signification of theatre as medium is not distinct from the technologies of its making' (Worthen, 2020: 9). When applied in performance, augmented and virtual reality have the potential to recalibrate the concept of theatre, while they themselves can acquire new properties and functions. Seen as 'a technological instrument that, as a representational medium, also represents the technologies it deploys as performance' (Worthen, 2020: 12), theatre can transform augmented and virtual reality into exciting spaces for play and imagination. This, in turn, has crucial implications for our understanding of the human as a spectator and a subject. According to Worthen, '[t]he theatre not only assimilates technologies; it represents their changing interface with theatre, and so with the technologized human' (Worthen, 2020: 28).

In foregrounding the notion of theatre as 'technicity', understood as 'the critique of the supplementary relation between notions of technology and the human', Worthen turns our attention 'to the ways theatre as an assemblage represents the human at the defining interface with technology' (Worthen, 2017: 321). Technology thus becomes a focal point for the exploration of human agency and subjectivity.

The relationship between humans and technology is a fundamental lens through which to discuss extended reality theatre, in which an audience member can acquire multiple roles by becoming a user, a participant, an immersant, and an experiencer. Robin Nelson argues that, in twenty-first-century theatre and media practice, the notion of the 'experiencer' might be introduced where the terms 'audience or even "spect-actor" (Boal) prove inadequate' because it might fit better with 'an environment designed to elicit a broadly visceral, sensual encounter, as distinct from conventional theatrical, concert or art gallery architectures which are constructed to draw primarily upon one of the sense organs – eyes (spectator) or ears (audience)' (Nelson, 2010: 45). His suggestion is particularly applicable to extended reality performances, in which the hybrids of physical and virtual environments introduce a range of sensory stimuli. Consequently, in this Element I will favour terms such as 'participant', 'immersant', and 'experiencer', though occasionally I will also use the terms 'audience' and 'spectator', given their popularity. At the same time, in emphasising perceptual shifts and sensory stimulation, I will follow Chiel Kattenbelt's argument about theatre as a hypermedium that 'can incorporate all media into its performance space' and in which 'very frequently the use of media technologies is to extend the lyrical and epical modes of representation for the sake of the intensity of the experience and the reflexivity of the thought' (Kattenbelt, 2006: 37). Although Kattenbelt's focus is on the concept of intermediality, his observations strongly resonate with the theory and practice of extended reality, in particular his claims that the combinations and co-relations of media can create new forms of perception and experience (Kattenbelt, 2008: 21, 25; Kattenbelt, 2010: 35).

In addressing the changing notion of theatre as a medium, the Element advances debates about the boundaries and possibilities of performance in the increasingly digitalised landscape of cultural production, as outlined, for example, by Sarah Bay-Cheng et al. (2015) and Matthew Causey (2016).

Stage practice has been rapidly and radically transformed in the twenty-first century through technological and social aspects of digital media. This Element provides a theoretical framework to explain what recent extended reality experiments might mean for our understanding and enjoyment of theatre, and for our appreciation of Shakespeare in particular. At the same time, the discussion addresses wider implications of extended reality for contemporary culture. As Bay-Cheng et al. have rightly noted, 'understanding the connections among media, technology, and performance has never been more vital. . . . Understanding these connections is thus not just a matter of theatre and performance studies, but necessary for a broader comprehension of contemporary culture' (Bay-Cheng et al., 2015: 2). Our grasp of contemporary culture would be incomplete without acknowledging the growing importance of augmented and virtual reality, which is changing our engagement with the arts, heritage, and entertainment.

One of the key issues concerning the application of technology in the twenty-first century has been what Henry Jenkins terms 'convergence culture', that is, 'the flow of content across multiple media platforms, the cooperation between multiple media industries, and the migratory behavior of media audiences who will go almost anywhere in search of the kinds of entertainment experiences they want' (Jenkins, 2006: 2). In the context of extended reality, the concept of convergence captures the possibility of moving between different kinds and combinations of realities in adapting the work for onstage and online formats. A good example of this is CREW's *Hamlet* project (2016–21), which had four iterations: a virtual reality installation *Hands-on-Hamlet* (2017); a live performance at KVS theatre in Brussels with virtual reality immersions, *Hamlet Encounters* (2018); a live theatre performance at KVS, *Hamlet's Lunacy* (2019), with elements of augmented and virtual reality; and an online performance, *Hamlet's Playground* (2021), on the platform Gather. In these distinctive iterations of the project, 360-degree videos and computer graphics were recycled for the purpose of each performance setting. Equally, each version has trialled different types of individual and communal experience for the participants, showing a broad range of dramaturgical forms that can be categorised under the category of extended reality.

Structure

The following exploration of extended reality in adaptations of Shakespeare is focused on three broad questions, each examined in a separate section. Section 1, 'What Is Extended Reality Shakespeare?', asks how we might define and categorise hybrid performances of Shakespeare as a new kind of theatre. According to Philipp A. Rauschnabel et al. (2022: 2), 'the meaning of the term or abbreviation "XR" remains ambiguous', with a number of competing and often contradictory definitions circulating within industry and academia. To address this issue, the section considers the physical–virtual spectrum to describe extended reality from technological and theatrical perspectives in order to offer a tailored taxonomy of extended reality Shakespeare adaptations that focuses on the audience experience.

Section 2, 'How Does It Work?', analyses selected examples of extended reality in Shakespeare's performances to test the proposed taxonomy in practice, but also to show how digital technologies can transform our understanding of the texts' themes and dramaturgical structures, and to identify different ways in which Shakespeare's works can support the development of extended reality in theatre. At the same time, the discussion reveals distinctive problems with adapting Shakespeare's language and plots into an extended reality format, with audiences struggling with the layering of physical and virtual environments, spatial disorientation, and abundance of stimuli alongside perceptual deprivation.

Finally, Section 3, 'What's the Future?', reflects on the promise of extended reality for revolutionising theatre practice and Shakespeare performance. It recognises exciting opportunities offered by digital technologies in terms of new forms of presence, embodiment, eventfulness, and interaction. However, it also acknowledges technological, dramaturgical, and institutional barriers faced by makers, users, and cultural programmers; overcoming them is a necessary step in finding ways forward. Ultimately, in seeking to define and document extended reality in Shakespeare performance, the Element aims to offer essential frameworks and tools to enable academics, practitioners, and general audiences better to understand this fascinating and fast-changing field.

1 What Is Extended Reality Shakespeare?

In March 2021, when the RSC released its *Dream*, an adaptation of Shakespeare's *A Midsummer Night's Dream*, it was clear that it had created something new. There was simply no vocabulary readily available to describe this production. Consequently, the artists and reviewers scrambled for the right words to articulate its hybrid and multi-layered nature. Actor Jamie Morgan, who played Peaseblossom, noted about the work that '[i]t crosses so many genres ... we're not even sure how to categorise it for ourselves', explaining further: 'When we're rehearsing, it feels like a piece of theatre. But then you feel like you're in a video game. I don't think anybody has worked on anything quite like this before' (cited in Hemming, 2021). Simultaneously, grappling with *Dream*'s experimental form, theatre reviewers adopted different approaches to introducing this piece. Louise Penn (2021) presented it matter-of-factly as a 'short show, using motion capture of actors, animation, music, and some audience interaction', whereas *The Guardian*'s Susannah Clapp described it poetically as a 'visual sprint' and 'a tumult of musical movement and images inspired by *A Midsummer Night's Dream*' (Clapp, 2021). Meanwhile, Alexis Soloski chose to explain it through negation: 'It isn't quite theater, and it isn't precisely film, though it could pass for a highbrow "Avatar" short. For stretches, it resembles a meditative video game, but it isn't that either, mostly because the interactive elements (clicking and dragging fireflies around the landscape) are wholly inconsequential' (Soloski, 2021). Ultimately, Peter Ormerod (2021) declared:

> A measure of its innovation is that the word does not yet exist to describe it. It is a live online broadcast featuring human performers transported to a computer-generated world partly controlled by the viewer; most of the music is prerecorded but some is played live. It's part theatre, part animation, part game; it feels excitingly like an experiment, but far warmer than that sounds.

Ormerod's lengthy description is to the point. As a show that engaged the actors and audiences in real time yet remotely and that featured performers live in a studio alongside avatars in a virtual reality environment, *Dream* could be easily neither categorised nor defined. It called for a new conceptual framework.

In this Element I examine *Dream* and other productions incorporating augmented and virtual reality as examples of extended reality theatre, positioning them in the context of vibrant debates on this topic. The aim of the section is to offer functional criteria for defining and describing hybrids of physical and digital environments in performances of Shakespeare to support their discussion, documentation, and design. Given both the novelty and the variety of technological and artistic approaches, the section provides key concepts and categories for capturing the distinctive ways in which such productions adapt the plays and engage the experiencers in the process of transforming their perceptions of the environment and their own bodies. The first part of the section ('Terminology versus Taxonomy') argues for the importance of taxonomy in the field of digital performance. The second part ('Insights and Inspirations') reviews three models that I consider relevant for developing a new taxonomy of extended reality performances of Shakespeare. Finally, the third part ('Taxonomy of Extended Reality Theatre') introduces and evaluates the proposed taxonomy, setting up the theoretical framework for the analysis of examples in Section 2.

Terminology versus Taxonomy

In foregrounding 'extended reality' as a term that is increasingly important in industry and academia, I aim to avoid terminological proliferation that is endemic in digital theatre and performance studies. According to Bay-Cheng et al., '[o]ne of the most consistent trends in the field is the coining of new terms and definitions to keep up with newly emerging technologies and practices. Contemporary researchers find themselves awash in numerous terms: *multimedia*, *digital performance*, *mixed-media performance*, *new media*, or as Lance Gharavi has half-jokingly termed it, "this kind of work"' (Bay-Cheng et al., 2015: 62–3, italics in original). Such proliferation stems from the focus on novelty among tech developers and thinkers but also from the genuine difficulty with capturing and categorising the constantly shifting field. The digital media discourse has to keep up with rapid technological developments as well as changing social attitudes and expectations. What is more, the discussion of the digital spans several disciplines: human–computer interactions, media studies, psychology, and performance studies, with each of them introducing its own concepts and frameworks. Finally, given that the digital media discourse is global and market driven, we are regularly introduced to new marketing nomenclatures since multinational corporations such as Apple, Meta Platforms, Inc. (formerly Facebook, Inc.), and Microsoft are keen to claim and control the language of the debate through their branding and rebranding strategies. The term 'metaverse', strongly promoted by Meta Platforms, Inc. as part of the company's global public relations campaign, is a striking example of this phenomenon.

Since the digital media discourse is constantly transforming and reinventing itself, concentrating on new terminology in this section and delivering yet another set of terms seems counterproductive. Instead, I propose to adopt a more systemic approach to extended reality theatre and to focus on taxonomy. Such an approach is also justified by the fact that even if we apply extended reality as a highly popular concept, we still have to acknowledge that it has no single definition that could be universally accepted in the human-centred computing community, let alone across different communities of users. Rauschnabel et al. (2022: 12) note that literature on this topic 'includes inconsistent and often conflicting conceptualizations . . ., resulting in confusion amongst academics, users, and practitioners'. Their findings make it perfectly clear that each time one discusses extended reality, one ought to reference an existing definition or provide a new one.

In this Element, extended reality is inscribed into a taxonomy of digital performance understood as a real-time socially interactive event. A range of foundational publications in different disciplines explore the central role of taxonomy in digital media discourse (e.g., Robinett, 1992; Milgram et al., 1994; Milgram and Kishino, 1994; Furht, 2011; Bay-Cheng et al., 2015; Rouse et al., 2015). These publications explicitly aim to define and categorise digital applications to establish foundations for further theoretical and practical research. For instance, in setting out to categorise all kinds of experience mediated by technology, Warren Robinett (1992: 230) explains that his taxonomy serves as 'a starting point for discussion'. Similarly, Bay-Cheng et al. argue that '[t]axonomies are not merely convenient systems for intellectual book-keeping. In every domain – biology, particle physics, political science, educational theory, art history, literary analysis, and performance studies – implicit and explicit taxonomies provide us with cognitive structures that shape the way we perceive and engage with the phenomena we investigate' (Bay-Cheng et al., 2015: 4). Designing a clear and functional taxonomy is thus a crucial step in the process of mapping the digital field.

At the same time, taxonomies are not unproblematic. They are not universal and fixed; rather, they are context-dependent and changeable. In assessing different definitions and taxonomies of mixed reality, Evan Barba et al. (2012: 929–30), for instance, note how each of them reflects its own technological and theoretical moment. What this suggests is that taxonomies, similarly to terminologies, are not immutable; on the contrary, they need to be regularly refined, repurposed, and, if necessary, replaced. Consequently, taxonomies, similarly to terminologies, can potentially proliferate to the point of creating confusion rather than clarity. What is more, given their importance for organising the discourse, taxonomies can be 'deeply coercive' (Bay-Cheng et al., 2015: 4) as they can impose rigid and restrictive modes of categorising information. In other words, taxonomies might explain but also constrain the reality that they describe.

To resolve these two major problems concerning taxonomies – their temporariness and their rigidity – one might apply them 'provisionally' and 'self-consciously' (Bay-Cheng et al., 2015: 4). This means embracing their dependence on specific technological and intellectual contexts. In this spirit, it is crucial to consider what objects are being categorised and what the primary function of a taxonomy is before designing a taxonomy, to make sure that it is appropriate and useful. With this in mind, I suggest that we consider two fundamental questions when developing a taxonomy in this section: (1) What is the taxonomy *of*? (2) What is the taxonomy *for*? Answering the first question is vital in that it brings to the foreground the specificity and the uniqueness of the objects that are under categorisation, so that the most suitable framework for their organisation can be devised. In this case, the decision to categorise augmented and virtual reality in performances of Shakespeare means that the focus should be not primarily on technological devices and their features but rather on distinctive dramaturgical set-ups and the users' experience of an event. Broadly speaking, the definition of extended reality underlying such a taxonomy should be adapted to the conditions and requirements of performance. Similarly, answering the second question is essential in terms of creating the structure of the taxonomy, so that it is fit for purpose and flexible. In this Element, given that extended reality performances of Shakespeare are being categorised to support their documentation, analysis, and production, it is necessary that we establish clear criteria for selection and comparison, making it possible to effectively map the field and offer useful tools for research and practice. Consequently, the proposed taxonomy should include those parameters that can bring together a range of theatrical works.

These considerations indicate that in developing the taxonomy of extended reality Shakespeare in performance we need to ensure that it meets a number of requirements. First, although such a taxonomy should be primarily experience-driven rather than technology-determined, in principle it still has to offer a consistent yet flexible framework for describing various technologies and formats. Consequently, I suggest that we include initially performances with augmented and virtual reality as the most evident examples of extended reality theatre, but that we also leave space for other (future) technologies, as long as they can enable the participants to experience hybrids of physical and virtual environments. In the near future, the development of volumetric capture and the 5G network might enable more sophisticated forms of dramaturgy, which could further expand the field of Shakespeare adaptation. The developments will enable novel effects of mirroring, doubling, contrasting, and blending between physical and virtual entities. As the users will be able to encounter representations of people, objects, and places in a three-dimensional format thanks to the improved speed, latency, and reliability of 5G, they will have a chance to explore varying degrees of interaction, proximity, and scale. This could enable, for instance, experiential explorations of the storm's metatheatricality in *The Tempest*, where the initial shipwreck might be embodied as a full-blown extended reality spectacle, and then it might be scaled down during Ariel's description of the storm.

Second, the taxonomy should enable comparisons of theatrical shows that apply multiple technologies within a single work. There are vastly different ways in which theatrical performances combine the physical with the virtual, so if we aim to document and study these varied arrangements in a responsive and representative manner, we need a system of organisation that is inclusive enough to accommodate a range of approaches. This is particularly important if we assume that hybrid environments are not necessarily dependent on a single dominant format, such as augmented or virtual reality; in fact, they might involve the participants moving within and between different kinds of environment in the course of performance.

Third, a taxonomy of extended reality theatre should capture the fundamental features of theatrical performance with immersive and interactive technologies that make them distinctive from other kinds of experience, such as virtual reality cinema, architectural design, and cultural heritage applications. Theatre is fundamentally based on some form of real-time interaction between actors and audiences or audiences as participants in a unique theatrical event that depends on liveness, and this aspect should be considered a distinguishing factor in discussions about theatrical expressions of extended reality. In this sense I agree with Kattenbelt when he argues that, '[u]nlike film and television, theatre always takes place in the absolute presence of here and now', although I do not insist that '[t]he performer and the spectator are physically present at the same time in the same space' (Kattenbelt, 2006: 33). I believe that it is possible for the performers and the experiencers or for the experiencers as a community of users to create other, mediated forms of co-presence in which they can still achieve the state described by Kattenbelt (2006: 33) as being 'there for each other'. Such a belief is supported by comments from theatre reviewers and by responses collected from the participants in a virtual reality *Hands-on-Hamlet* installation by CREW and in an augmented reality *Tempest* performance by Nexus. The users of these experiences insisted on the need for acknowledgement, agency, and interaction, which 'testifies to the power of physically co-present live performance as a model for VR and AR, but equally to the difficulty of transcending this model to radically re-imagine mixed reality theatre' (Mancewicz, 2023: 108). At the same time, similarly to Kattenbelt, I acknowledge that theatre incorporates other media, particularly as it negotiates its position in the dynamic landscape of technology and culture. In emphasising both theatre's distinctness and its entanglement with other media, I draw on Kattenbelt's notion of theatre as a hypermedium, that is, 'a medium that can contain all media', and thus it functions as 'a stage for intermediality' (Kattenbelt, 2008: 23). Seen from this perspective, theatre, according to Claudia Georgi, has the 'ability to integrate other media without affecting their respective materiality and mediality' (Georgi, 2014: 46); it can provide a space for different media combinations and cross-overs within its own media framework. This also presupposes an idea of media specificities and media boundaries. As Georgi notes, '[a]lthough media relate to each other and need to be analysed in comparison to each other, they are nevertheless distinct and have their specific characteristics' (Georgi, 2014: 10). The observation is particularly relevant for theatre in extended reality, where the audiences might be craving well-recognisable conventions and patterns of reception. Such media-specific features might help the experiencers orientate themselves more easily in an unfamiliar set-up of novel media and technologies.

These three requirements as just listed will inform the development of an extended reality taxonomy of theatre in this section. At the same time, the categorisation will not emerge in a vacuum; rather, it will draw on existing models and discussions.

Insights and Inspirations

In designing the taxonomy of theatrical adaptations of Shakespeare, I draw on three existing models: (1) the Reality–Virtuality (RV) Continuum (Milgram et al., 1994; Milgram and Kishino, 1994), (2) an MR versus MR^x model (Rouse et al., 2015), and (3) the Material-Mediated Performance Spectrum (Bay-Cheng, 2015). What brings them together and makes them particularly useful is that they all explicitly incorporate the notion of hybridity understood as the combination of physical and virtual environments. In this section, I explore the assumptions and insights emerging from these models, while evaluating them as inspirations for developing a taxonomy of extended reality theatre.

The first model, the RV Continuum, focuses on mixed reality visual displays, but since its publication it has served as a principal framework for understanding mixed reality in multiple disciplines, ranging from human–computer interactions to theatre studies. What is perhaps the most appealing about the work of Paul Milgram, Haruo Takemura, Akira Utsumi, and Fumio Kishino is that, at least on the surface, they offer relatively simple and basic concepts that can be adapted in different contexts. Milgram and Kishino explain, for instance, that 'the most straightforward way to view a Mixed Reality environment . . . is [as] one in which real world and virtual world objects are presented together within a single display, that is, anywhere between the extrema of the virtuality continuum' (Milgram and Kishino, 1994: 3). Their continuum, while based on various types of display, focuses on different combinations of physical and virtual environments that are enabled by these displays, as shown in Figure 2.

A version of this model first appeared in Milgram and Kishino (1994: 3), and it was revised in the publication by Milgram et al. (1994: 283), with the 'virtuality continuum' becoming the 'Reality–Virtuality Continuum'. It is the updated model that I will discuss in this section since I find it to be more precise and accurate. The concept of the continuum is central here, so I will explore it now in more detail.

First, the continuum suggests that the phenomena on the two extreme ends, the real environment and the virtual environment, are not necessarily

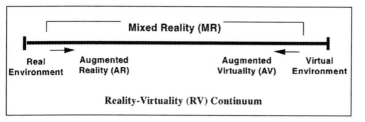

Figure 2 The *RV Continuum* by Milgram et al. (1994: 283).

contrasting but rather complementary categories. Milgram et al. define the real environment as 'constrained by the laws of physics' and the virtual environment as 'one in which the participant-observer is totally immersed in a completely synthetic world' (Milgram et al., 1994: 283). They explain that the 'synthetic world . . . may or may not mimic the properties of a real-world environment, either existing or fictional, but . . . may also exceed the bounds of physical reality by creating a world in which the physical laws governing gravity, time and material properties no longer hold' (Milgram et al., 1994: 283). However, in the context of mixed reality and indeed also extended reality, as the two concepts are understood in this Element, the physical and the synthetic elements might be defined not so much by their differences as by their similarities, since they emerge as alternative models of the world's organisation and the user's perception. In fact, as Milgram et al. note, '[r]ather than regarding the two concepts simply as antitheses . . . it is more convenient to view them as lying at opposite ends of a *continuum*' (Milgram et al., 1994: 283). What is even more important, Milgram and Kishino argue that there being 'subtle differences in interpreting the two terms ['the real' and 'the virtual'] is not as critical, since the basic intention there is that a "virtual" world be synthesised, by computer, to give the participant the impression that that world is not actually artificial but is "real", and that the participant is "really" present within that world' (Milgram and Kishino, 1994: 6). The environments on the opposite ends of the RV Continuum are thus both designed to feel real to the participants, which has prompted me in this Element to avoid juxtaposing the terms 'the real' and 'the virtual' as heterogenous or even contrasting concepts. Instead, I refer to combinations of the physical and the virtual (or digital) environments. Despite different terminology, in accentuating the analogies rather than the differences, Milgram and Kishino offer a way out of a strict dichotomy between the real and the virtual, since such dichotomy has become untenable in today's digitalised and networked society. They also emphasise the ways in which different kinds of environment ultimately aim to offer the participant a sense of presence, the feeling of being here and now. This sense of presence is crucial when we discuss extended reality theatre as it indicates the potential of virtual environments to function as meeting places for performers and immersants.

Second, the continuum implies that the phenomena on the opposite sides do not necessarily represent their respective categories as pure entities. Instead, we could interpret these phenomena as parameters for comparison. Again, seen from this perspective, the continuum invites fundamental revision of the ways in which we understand terms such as 'virtuality' and 'reality'. Milgram and Kishino observe 'that the VR label is also frequently used in association with a variety of other environments, to which total immersion and complete synthesis do not necessarily pertain, but which fall somewhere along a virtuality continuum' (Milgram and Kishino, 1994: 2). Similarly, Joris Weijdom reminds us that virtual reality as a term 'doesn't acknowledge a certain mix, and implies that the experience of a "total virtual reality", without the physical body, could actually exist' (Weijdom, 2017: 7). A more accurate account of virtual reality is one that recognises the location of the participant in the space and the significance of proprioception and embodiment for the virtual experience. In fact, as Roberts-Smith notes, 'perceptual submersion does not hinge on the degree to which a VR system *excludes* sensory stimuli, but on the degree to which it *includes* stimuli participants expect to encounter in the real world', pointing to 'representational fidelity', 'interactivity', and 'identity construction' as key factors in which the real underpins the experience of the virtual (Roberts-Smith, 2021: 6). An example of a virtual reality performance that emphasises location and embodiment is *Current, Rising*, directed by Netia Jones at the Royal Opera House, scheduled for 2020 and postponed to 2021 owing to Covid-19 restrictions. Described by its creators as 'the world's first opera in hyper reality' (Oliver, 2020), this loose adaptation of *The Tempest* combines virtual reality immersion with a multisensory experience of the set. Given that, ontologically, opera and theatre share fundamental similarities as forms of representative live performance, I have included this production in the Element. Most importantly, in recognition of virtual reality's reliance on space and the body, I argue for its inclusion in the category of extended reality experiences.

Finally, the continuum shows that there is a range of different phenomena in between the established categories and that one can move on the scale as part of the experience. There might be examples that merge certain categories as well as examples that blend and blur them. To address these cases, Milgram and Kishino propose 'the term *"Hybrid Reality"* (HR) as a way of encompassing the concept of blending many types of distinct display media'; they further suggest that such displays might be defined as 'Hyberspace' (Milgram and Kishino, 1994: 4, italics in original). Their notion of hybridity involves especially '[c]ompletely graphic' environments to which real elements are added either through 'video "reality"' or through 'physical objects' that can be manipulated by users (Milgram and Kishino, 1994: 4). What is more, Weijdom argues that mixed reality, understood in the sense of extended reality as the term is applied here, is not only about all kinds of hybrid and indeterminate cases; it is also about the cases moving on the continuum, particularly in the context of theatre: 'The MR experience of a participating audience can shift back and forth on this scale [i.e. on the continuum introduced by Milgram et al.] for the duration of a piece, and can cover a wider or smaller range within any given production' (Weijdom, 2017: 7). The RSC *Dream* is a perfect example of this, with the audience experiencing different degrees of physical and virtual input during the performance. It is also because of these shifts that it is difficult to find one specific term to describe this production, while the taxonomy with a continuum scale might offer a more comprehensive framework for capturing the audience experience. Bay-Cheng (2015: 47–8) proposes another example of such shifting. It is the project MagicBook from 2001, which can be read like a physical object but can also be enhanced through applications of augmented and virtual reality. As such, the project 'does not sit neatly at one end of the spectrum, but occupies several places simultaneously' (Bay-Cheng, 2015: 48); consequently, it 'can be seen to span the whole of the Reality–Virtuality Continuum' (Holz et al., 2011: 254). Because of its versatility, MagicBook 'demonstrates the necessity of developing further this spectrum to account for simultaneous and somewhat contradictory elements' (Bay-Cheng, 2015: 48). These remarks suggest the need for revising the model designed by Milgram and his collaborators to account for the dynamic and complex nature of theatre with augmented and virtual reality.

Given that the emphasis of the RV Continuum is on broader implications of technology rather than on technology itself, the model continues to be relevant despite the changes in software and hardware; it is also referenced across different contexts and sectors. In this section, it inspires the design of the extended reality taxonomy as a spectrum. However, since the RV Continuum focuses on visual displays, its finer details are of limited use in other fields, for instance in theatre and performance studies. Most importantly, the three dimensions of visual displays proposed by Milgram et al. – Extent of World Knowledge (EWK), Reproduction Fidelity (RF), and Extent of Presence Metaphor (EPM) (Milgram et al., 1994: 287–91) – are not really applicable across different disciplines, unless they were to be substantially adapted. Consequently, they have not been nearly as influential in the discussions of extended reality as the RV Continuum. What it shows is that in a rapidly developing field of technology, models that emphasise specific devices and their functions can quickly become obsolete. At the same time, it indicates that we need a tailored system of categorisation to account for the uniqueness of theatre and performance in extended reality.

The next two models that I propose to use as insights and inspirations represent a theatrical perspective. The MR^x model introduced by Rebecca Rouse, Maria Engberg, Nassim JafariNaimi, and Jay David Bolter complements the continuum model of mixed reality designed by Milgram and his collaborators. It highlights the applications of MR^x considering two factors: the application's purpose (whether it focuses on experience or transfer of information) and the use of space or place (whether it is located in space or integrated into a place), as shown in Figure 3.

The diagram aims to foreground the distinctness of MR^x from MR. As Rouse et al. explain, '[w]e designate these applications MR^x to distinguish them from the broader category of MR. The superscript x is meant to mark the importance of user experience in the configuration of this new class of applications. MR^x applications are designed to be engaging experiences, not primarily . . . tools for accomplishing tasks' (Rouse et al., 2015: 178). In the diagram, while all four quadrants represent mixed reality as a more general category, only the upper two refer to MR^x. In underlining the importance of the user's experience, Rouse et al. (2015) are interested in the social and cultural aspects of mixed reality. This means that they give only secondary importance to technology, unlike Milgram et al. (1994), who, as mentioned, expanded their model with three dimensions of visual displays: EWK, RF, and EPM. Thus, although Rouse and her collaborators draw on computer

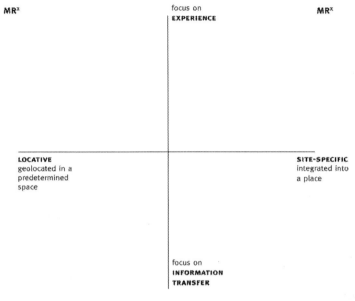

Figure 3 An MR versus MR[x] model by Rouse et al. (2015).

science in defining mixed reality quite broadly as 'the wide range of applications that situate digital information in the world (Rouse et al., 2015: 177), their description of MR[x] is more user-focused. They see MR[x] as those applications that in '[t]heir design goals may include entertainment, personal expression, informal education, or collective action (for example, through social media) among others' (Rouse et al., 2015: 178). To further distinguish MR[x] applications within the broader category of mixed reality, Rouse et al. present them as 'hybrid, deeply locative and often site-specific, and esthetic, performative, and/or social' (Rouse et al., 2015: 178). All these qualities are inherently linked with the user's experience. For instance, when 'MR[x] applications seek to combine the physical and the virtual into an effective hybrid', they do so 'for the sake of the experience' (Rouse et al., 2015: 178).

Ultimately, the focus on experience leads to the development of 'a humanistic framework' (Rouse et al., 2015: 178) in which three different disciplines, namely, media studies, performance studies, and design studies, provide distinctive lenses for viewing MR^x. The most helpful for the task of designing the MR taxonomy of theatre is a performance studies lens. As Rouse explains:

> Performance studies and theatre history in combination provide a unique viewpoint on practices of site-specificity and physical-media hybridity. This perspective not only provides tools for analysis of examples, but also direction for the design process, in terms of emphasis on the relationship of site and experience as a whole, integration of physical and mediated elements, and consideration of the role or roles played by spectators, participants, actors and others. (Rouse, 2015: 205)

The performance studies lens underlines the importance of space as a site of experience. It turns MR^x into 'a performative and theatrical stage' (Rouse, 2015: 195) in which the users enter into strong relationships with the site, often in a site-specific manner. Frequently in MR^x applications the users are able to co-create and transform the site. Their participation is enabled by both technological and cultural changes. As Rouse explains, the possibility to influence one's experience 'is due to both the availability of less expensive, more accessible interactive technologies such as mobile phones and sensors like the Kinect, as well as the increasing acceptance and interest in participation as an aesthetic' (Rouse, 2015: 205). The user's ability to interact with the site, and potentially alter it, is an important element in the model developed by Rouse et al. (2015).

At the same time, the focus on space and place and on the distinction between locative versus site-specific examples is not necessarily of key relevance for most performances that apply augmented and virtual reality. In fact, none of the examples discussed here is site-specific in the sense of responding to a particular place and defining itself through relationship with it. None would fit with Nick Kaye's evocative description that '[t]o move the site-specific work is to *re-place* it, to make it *something else*' (Kaye, 2000: 2). This means that although the diagram is revolutionary in its acknowledgement of MR^x as a performance space, its emphasis on site-specificity suits better those examples that belong to visual art and architecture. The versatility of the model thus constitutes both its strength and its weakness. On the one hand, Rouse et al. (2015) make it possible to compare MR^x experiences across different disciplines, showing how the hybrids of the physical and the virtual can lead to a diverse range of set-ups. On the other hand, an interdisciplinary framework does not fully account for the specificity of theatre as a medium. Indeed, the examples examined by Rouse (2015) represent two categories that are not obviously aligned with the distinctive features of theatre. The first one is 'MR^x Architectural Screens', which are 'experiences in which a built environment or building that has a normal use that is not screenal is transformed into a dynamic projection surface by projection mapping or other technologies'; the second one is 'MR^x Exhibits and Tours', in which participants go on a journey through a space, often completing a series of tasks with an educational purpose (Rouse, 2015: 198). In each case, it is not necessary that the experience has an element of social interaction, as the emphasis is placed on the relationship between the work and its location.

An attention to theatre and performance is what distinguishes the final model discussed as an insight and an inspiration in this section, that is, the Material-Mediated Performance Spectrum proposed by Bay-Cheng (2015). The model covers a broad range of media uses in performance; as such it does not directly reference extended reality. It is, however, invaluable since Bay-Cheng selects three categories that are fundamentally theatrical: space, time, and bodies. At the same time, as in the model by Milgram et al. (1994), these three categories are stretched between the physical and the virtual (or, in this case, between the material and the mediated) as two extreme poles, as shown in Figure 4, with Bay-Cheng foregrounding the nature of her model as a continuum.

The categories in this model are based on the traditional understanding of theatre as a meeting of actors and audience members. At the same time, they are presented from a critical perspective. As Bay-Cheng notes, 'these three categories remain fundamental to performance practice, even (and perhaps

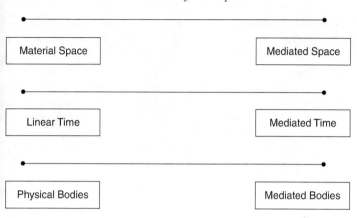

Figure 4 Material-Mediated Performance Spectrum by Bay-Cheng (2015).

especially) when they are challenged' (Bay-Cheng, 2015: 46). She explains further that '[m]edia-performance intersections are frequently noted for their potential to radically reorganize space (e.g., telematics, live feeds, and virtual or augmented reality), time (e.g., prerecorded material, flashbacks, simultaneous action), and bodies (e.g., cyborgs, robots, prosthetics, extreme body modification)' (Bay-Cheng, 2015: 46). It is thus precisely by examining the major challenges to these three categories that we can capture the extent of transformation that digital media bring to theatre.

Crucially, in Bay-Cheng's taxonomy, this transformation is represented in terms of distortion. The scholar notes that we have 'a conceptual ideal' that consists in 'an unmediated materiality, reality, or "nature" as Einstein claimed,' which 'all performance – and indeed all representation' inevitably distorts (Bay-Cheng, 2015: 46). In this context, live theatre and digital media are not in opposition; rather, they can be placed on a scale from the material to the mediated, very much like visual displays are placed on a continuum from the real to the virtual in the model proposed by Milgram and his collaborators. Moreover, as in the case of the RV Continuum, each end of the scale on the Material-Mediated Performance Spectrum represents an absolute degree of either physicality or mediatisation, although Bay-Cheng describes the two extreme ends as 'unattainable ideals' (Bay-Cheng, 2015: 49). Their principal purpose is to establish the concepts for comparison, so that audience members might place a particular performance, or even a particular moment in a performance, somewhere on the scale in each of the three fundamental categories: space, time, and bodies. This subjective approach is what Bay-Cheng deems to be the 'greatest conceptual advantage' of her model and 'the basis for the future of the project online', in which different spectators might be able to input their responses, contributing to a collective and dynamic database of performance (Bay-Cheng, 2015: 63). Such a solution enables analysis of different mediatised moments within a single performance as well as comparisons across a number of works. Consequently, what Bay-Cheng's model offers to the taxonomy of extended reality theatre is, on the one hand, consideration of theatrical categories and, on the other, focus on audience experience. Both these elements will underline the taxonomy proposed in this section. At the same time, it would be difficult to adapt Bay-Cheng's model with its three variable dimensions to classify an emerging field; instead, a simpler structure might be easier to use. I hope to achieve this by foregrounding digital works as hybrid entities and limiting the number of variables. Similarly to Rouse et al. (2015), I believe that performances in extended reality radically transform our experience of space, which should be placed at the centre of discussion. However, although I agree with Bay-Cheng that the real-time immediacy and the interactivity of the performance constitute other crucial dimensions, I suggest that we include them as necessary requirements rather than variables on the scale. Next I explain the model in more detail.

Taxonomy of Extended Reality Theatre

The taxonomy of extended reality theatre proposed here draws on the principles of hybridity and continuum, which are common to all three of the taxonomies discussed in the previous subsection. While the scale stretches from the physical to the virtual as two extreme points, the range of extended reality theatre falls from performances in predominantly physical space with some virtual elements to performances in predominantly virtual space with some physical elements, with works that balance physical

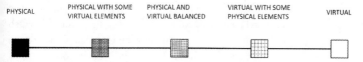

Figure 5 Proposed taxonomy of extended reality theatre.

and virtual elements (in more or less equal measure) placed in the middle, as shown in Figure 5.

Such a set-up underlines hybridity as a necessary condition of extended reality theatre, making it clear that there has to be a certain degree of interplay between the physical and the virtual elements for a particular production to be placed in this range. Each point within the range thus underlines some form of contamination and confluence.

At the same time, the focus on space evokes the MR versus MR^x model in which the user explores, experiences, and potentially even transforms their environment, as well as the Material-Mediated Performance Spectrum, in which space is one of the three critical dimensions. However, unlike the Material-Mediated Performance Spectrum, the taxonomy involves only one variable dimension, although it assumes real-time eventness and social inter-activity as requirements.

Space is hybrid in the sense of direct links between physical and virtual environments, both of which need to be experienced by the audience. Such an understanding of extended reality theatre is narrower than Benford and Giannachi's definition of mixed reality, which includes examples such as Blast Theory's *Can You See Me Now?*, where the participants joining online and the participants on the streets occupied two separate spaces that were connected to form 'an *adjacent reality* rather than augmented reality, which in its ideal tries to seamlessly connect one world to another' (Benford et al., 2006: 108). What is more, the hybrid space in extended reality theatre tends to be shared by the actors and the spectators or the spectators as participants, creating distinctive opportunities for interaction, collaboration, and collectivity.

To further underline the notions of interaction, collaboration, and collectivity, the taxonomy assumes that the productions are happening in real time, which means that the users experience them as communal events that have been scheduled to happen on specific dates with set performance times. The synchronous dimension ensures the notion of 'eventness', which Willmar Sauter defines as central to theatre as a medium that, as he argues, 'manifests itself as an event which includes both the presentation of actions and the reactions of the spectators, who are present at the very moment of the creation. Together the actions and reactions constitute the theatrical event' (Sauter, 2000: 11). The synchronous and simultaneous nature of extended reality theatre ensures that it can bring several people together, allowing them to become participants but also witnesses of a temporary collective. When the RSC *Dream* premiered in March 2021, a year since the introduction of the UK's strict lockdown, it attracted over its initial nine-day run thousands of spectators who were eager to participate in the communal and interactive experience. Once the show became available just for viewing – without actors performing live at set times, without the option of audience interaction, and without the post-show discussion – public interest in the production declined dramatically.

This brings us to the third key element of extended reality theatre, which is social interaction. According to Maximilian Speicher et al., '[i]nteraction is a key aspect in MR, which can be divided into implicit and explicit . . . . While all types of MR require implicit interaction, e.g., walking around a virtual object registered in space, explicit interaction means intentionally providing input to, e.g., manipulate the MR scene' (Speicher et al., 2019: 10). What is striking about these observations is that they articulate some but not all aspects of interaction in extended reality theatre, and they omit the most crucial ones. Extended reality performances involve not only audience members making implicit and explicit interventions within the space (ideally in ways that make their effects visible to others) but also actors relating to the audience, and audience members relating to each other. Ultimately, the interactions are designed to create a sense of communal experience that is embedded within the performance content. The limited run combined with the variable and unpredictable effects of interactivity means that extended reality performances are ephemeral, unavailable on demand, and inimitable, with each iteration being unlike any other.

The proposed emphasis on eventness and social interaction as defining categories of extended reality performance adapts Erika Fischer-Lichte's formula, in which 'performances are generated and determined by a self-referential and ever-changing feedback loop' (Fischer-Lichte, 2008: 38). According to her account, 'whatever the actors do elicits a response from the spectators, which impacts on the entire performance', making it 'unpredictable and spontaneous to a certain degree' (Fischer-Lichte, 2008: 38). In Fischer-Lichte's formula, this kind of 'feedback loop' involves the actors and audiences being physically present in the same space at the same time, breathing the same air and having direct, unmediated impact on each other. In such a scenario, 'the spectators laugh, cheer, sigh, groan, sob, cry, scuff their feet, or hold their breath; they yawn, fall asleep, and begin to snore; they cough and sneeze, eat and drink, crumple wrapping paper, whisper, or shout comments, call "bravo" and "encore," applaud, jeer and boo, get up, leave the theatre, and bang the door on their way out' (Fischer-Lichte, 2008: 38). This, in turn, affects the actors as their 'voices get louder and unpleasant or, alternatively, more seductive; they feel animated to invent gags, to improvise, or get distracted and miss a cue; they step closer to the lights to address the audience directly or ask them to calm down, or even to leave the theatre' (Fischer-Lichte, 2008: 38). In extended reality performances, on the other hand, the interactions tend to be mediatised (in the sense of being mediated by technology). This might be because the actors and the audiences are encountering each other as avatars in a virtual environment rather than as bodies in a physical venue. Similarly, the interventions in the space might be virtual rather than physical, allowing audience members to manifest their presence or experience the presence of others through digital traces, without the (simultaneous) presence of the actors.

Enabling a virtual version of the feedback loop, extended reality performances thus revisit 'the specific mediality of performance', which, according to Max Hermann, 'consists of the bodily co-presence of actors and spectators' (cited in Fischer-Lichte, 2008: 38). In extended reality theatre, being as bodies and being physically co-present as actors and spectators are not the necessary conditions of performance as a medium; they are only some of the ways in which the work can create a feedback loop. What ultimately distinguishes extended reality theatre is its ability to offer the audience the perception of co-presence, as it is facilitated by advanced tracking and mapping technologies. It is not about actually

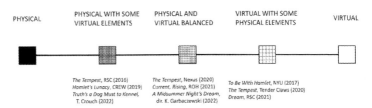

Figure 6 Proposed taxonomy of extended reality Shakespeare adaptations.

being together but about giving the participants the feeling of togetherness and interactivity, in a recycled, reinvented version of the theatre's traditional formula of *hic et nunc*, here and now.

In presenting real-time interaction as a necessary condition of extended reality performance, the proposed taxonomy thus places the experiencers firmly at the centre. It shows that they are not only negotiating their positions and roles within a hybrid space; they are also involved in multiple acts of individual and collective world-building. At the same time, the focus on real-time interactions and on the shared experience of space puts limitation on what is categorised as an extended reality performance. Such limitation, however, is crucial in terms of enabling the creation of a coherent data set. Given that the focus of this Element is on augmented and virtual reality adaptations of Shakespeare, I present in Figure 6 a selection of such examples within my proposed taxonomy.

Not all of these examples are straightforward cases of augmented and virtual reality. The RSC's *The Tempest* and Tim Crouch's *Truth's a Dog Must to Kennel*, for instance, do not involve any devices for the audience. In the first case, however, the three-dimensional motion-captured projection of Ariel (played by Mark Quartley) creates an effect of augmented reality. In Crouch's performance, in turn, the performer equipped in a virtual reality headset 'deceptively void of all VR technology' (Crouch, 2022: 2) invites the audience to imagine with him what he could be seeing as a virtual immersion. This shows that the selection is to some extent subjective. Still, I hope that it will facilitate further documentation and research. Given that many of these extended reality works originated at university labs or in experimental studios and circulated as prototypes, their public dissemination and discussion is crucial. At the same time, the accumulation of examples from 2020 and 2021 – accounting for four of the nine examples presented in this Element – underlines the vital role of the Covid-19 pandemic in introducing extended reality theatre to mainstream audiences.

Finally, the list brings me back to the three requirements for the taxonomy of extended reality theatre that I identified earlier, and that I propose to use as criteria for evaluating the efficacy of the proposed model. The first one is that the taxonomy should be both consistent and flexible to accommodate a range of technologies and set-ups. Indeed, the model is not bound to any specific tools and formats, particularly if they were to radically change or disappear. Given the dynamic development of the field, there might well be new modes of experiencing immersion and interactivity in the future, and perhaps the very concepts of augmented, virtual, and mixed reality will be no longer relevant, replaced by a broader understanding of extended reality. Indeed, the growing popularity of extended reality as a label is an indication of a paradigm shift in the field.

Second, the taxonomy should make it possible to compare productions in which different kinds of technology are used in a single performance. Given that the examples are situated on the continuum of spatial hybrids, the list can include productions such as CREW's *Hamlet's Lunacy*, which combines augmented and virtual reality within a live theatre production. Since the only variable in the taxonomy concerns the use of space, this particular dimension functions as a marker for categorising different examples on the continuum.

Third, the taxonomy should enable media comparisons through setting up distinctions between different immersive experiences, such as theatrical performances, cinema, gaming, and architectural design. A test case for this might be Boston's Commonwealth Shakespeare Company's *Hamlet 360: Thy Father's Spirit* (2019), directed by Steven Maler and produced in collaboration with Google and Sensorium. This 360-degree recording allows viewers to freely change their viewpoint of the space, which has led Rebecca W. Bushnell and Michael Ullyot (2022: 39–41) to examine it as a mixture of theatrical and cinematic strategies. *Hamlet 360* did not have a set performance run, but it has been freely available on YouTube, with audiences able to virtually enter the piece, pause it, and replay it at any point. While these features are immensely helpful in terms of the work's accessibility, they also mean that it is likely to be viewed as an immersive film rather than a performance event, particularly since the users cannot interact with the actors or each other. It is for these reasons that the proposed taxonomy includes socially interactive works as events, since the possibility of sharing the experience and responding to it together introduces elements of community-building and world-building. The two dimensions thus make it possible to establish clearer distinctions between cinema and theatre in virtual reality.

Conclusion

Taxonomies are practical tools for organising the world, but they are also conceptual constructs that encourage reflection on essential characteristics of objects. Devising a taxonomy of extended reality theatre means deciding not only what we define as extended reality but also, and perhaps more importantly, what we recognise as theatre and how we understand performance as well as its relationship to audiences, other media, and the world more broadly. Thomas Postlewait and Tracy C. Davis have persuasively shown that 'the meaning of theatricality cannot be taken for granted' (Postlewait and Davis, 2003: 2), but the observation extends also to the meaning of theatre as a medium. Indeed, Samuel Webber explicitly interrogates the changing role of theatre and theatricality in an electronic age, noting the growing importance and proliferation of '[t]heatrical practices, attitudes, even organisations' (Webber, 2004: 1). Shakespeare-oriented, digital research and practice is a good example of this trend as it shows how well-established, more traditional forms of performance are being evoked to examine our position in networked models of culture and society.

Our understanding of what constitutes a theatrical performance has evolved over the centuries in terms of spatial set-ups and audience–actor configurations; however, it is the arrival of extended reality technologies that has brought a radical transformation of theatre's ability to give audiences the feeling of being present. At the same time, while extended reality can redefine the key characteristics of performance, it also exposes our long-held perceptions and expectations of theatre. As Weijdom points out, 'VR and AR experiences are live, embodied and performative; terms that the theatre is very familiar with. Also, they deal with designed mixes of real and virtual spaces, and question our perception of reality and our understanding of presence. These are again concepts that the theatre has been dealing with for at least a few hundred years' (Weijdom, 2017: 7). Re-examining these concepts from the perspective of extended reality is important not only in terms of updating our definition of theatre but also in terms of reconsidering what we have meant by theatre in the first place.

Similarly, in the area of staging Shakespeare, the advancement of digital productions makes us re-evaluate the idea of live Shakespeare performance and Shakespeare as a source. According to Yong Li Lan, '[a]s electronic Shakespeare circulates in hyperspace, our practices of knowing and producing Shakespeare now appear sharply implicated in the concrete forms, materials and institutional structures of a particular medium once it is compared to the fluidity, the disembodiedness, and the decentralization of the electronic one' (Li Lan, 2003: 46). As Shakespeare's digital presence intensifies, his works increasingly function as open-source material. A good example of this is the British Council's Mix the Play, an interactive, intuitive video platform that allows users to choose and apply film effects to create a scene and then share it on social media, deciding on casting, costume, music, and so on. In the iteration created by the accomplished Indian director and playwright Roysten Abel, users could stage their own version of *Romeo and Juliet*. Designed to make Shakespeare's dramas more attractive to young people, Mix the Play turns the texts into free sampling material, responding to contemporary fascination with recycling, customisation, and social media virality.

An effort to articulate what constitutes theatre and Shakespeare against the backdrop of the ever-expanding spectrum of physical and virtual hybrids is thus necessarily implicated in dominant cultural tendencies and industry developments. It also means undertaking a double task. On the one hand we have to acknowledge the legacy of theatre as one of the oldest and most culturally established media, and on the other we need to assess its potential to appropriate emerging tools and technologies. In this context, extended reality performances of Shakespeare have a particularly important role to play. In the West, Shakespeare has become synonymous with theatre, and he has been praised for his intimate understanding of the stage and the spectators. Artists appropriating his plays in the extended reality mode are testing the potential of cutting-edge digital tools for making Shakespeare's work more accessible for twenty-first-century audiences. At the same time, Shakespeare's dramas offer exciting insights into the nature of performance as an act of illusion-making and world-building, which can be inspiring to artists experimenting with augmented and virtual reality. In Section 2, I propose to examine examples of extended reality Shakespeare adaptations that occupy a thrilling intersection of text, theatre, and technology.

2 How Does It Work?

Extended reality comes in so many forms that perhaps no one production is like any other. In each case, different kinds of environment are engaged, layered, and interwoven through unique technological and dramaturgical set-ups. In adaptations of Shakespeare's plays, each example is also an exceptional encounter of early modern dramaturgy with twenty-first-century digital tools. What brings these performances together is that they can all enrich the experiencers' perception of presence, proprioception, and embodiment, enabling them to inhabit a mixture of physical and virtual worlds. They also tend to accentuate the moments of magic and metatheatre in Shakespeare's sources. At the same time, as each performance results from an effort to solve specific theatrical and technological challenges, each brings us closer to understanding the potential of augmented and virtual reality for making theatre.

While Section 1 aimed at capturing the distinguishing characteristics of extended reality theatre by offering a taxonomy of extended reality adaptations of Shakespeare, in this section I test the proposed model by showing how several works might exemplify the three distinctive spatial configurations: physical space with some virtual elements, physical and virtual spaces blended more or less equally, and virtual space with some physical elements. The division into categories is to some extent subjective and flexible as it is the experiencer who serves here as a point of reference, while the works fall into a scale within and between the categories. In each case, however, as a result of an extended reality set-up, the experiencer might witness and/or embody the layering of realities and modes of representation, resulting in the fundamental transformation of space, which becomes both *the space of performance* and *the space performed*.

To describe this process, but also to demonstrate the challenges of adapting different Shakespeare plays for extended reality, the section mentions several productions and offers substantial analysis of three examples, one per spatial configuration. The three examples have been chosen to showcase distinctive technological and textual solutions. These are also the works that I have personally experienced, which allows me to comment on their user design and emotional impact. Incidentally, all three productions were affected by the Covid-19 pandemic and the lockdown, though each in its own way. CREW's *Hamlet's Lunacy* was subsequently transformed into *Hamlet's Playground* to be performed on a digital platform, Gather. The Royal Opera House's *Current, Rising* was postponed by half a year because of lockdown restrictions. Finally, the RSC's *Dream* was redesigned to be performed online after the production planned to premiere live in Stratford had to be cancelled.

The discussion of examples in this section focuses on contaminations, crossovers, and contrasts between physical and virtual environments as they are experienced or embodied by audiences in stagings of Shakespeare's texts. What is crucial about the examined works is that the creation of realistic representation and perfect illusion is rarely their ultimate goal. Instead, they shift and question the experiencers' awareness of their own bodies and their positions in the space by overwhelming, repositioning, and disorienting the senses. In particular, the performances examined here underline the idea of virtual reality as an embodied experience, which in turn justifies the inclusion of fully immersive virtual reality works. According to Roberts-Smith, the emphasis on embodiment is a vital condition for understanding the virtual environment: 'If we conceive of VR experiences as situated in each individual participant's body and incorporating the unique and unpredictable contingencies that each individual brings with them, we will necessarily acknowledge and encourage a much broader range of perceptions than a hermetically "immersive" system can accommodate' (Roberts-Smith, 2021: 7). She further argues that '[i]n addition to enriching opportunities for meaning-making, this approach also opens new possibilities for representation in virtual worlds, which need no longer be tied to realism' (Roberts-Smith, 2021: 7). The emphasis on the body and the senses can thus be used to create novel forms of world-building, but also to fore-ground the acts of representation, perception, and presence. Shakespeare's plays provide rich material for such exploration, given their metatheatrical interrogation of acting as an interplay of appearance and truth.

At the same time, the focus on embodiment invites more complex combinations of realities and more critically informed experiences. As Nele Wynants et al. note in relation to the work of CREW, 'we would no longer describe the embodied environment in terms of virtual as opposed to real, but as a transitional space in between different levels of perceived reality' (Wynants et al., 2008: 161). According to Wynants et al., '[i]t is in this shifting moment between the embodied and the perceived world, on the fracture between what we see and what we feel that the spectator has the strongest feeling of being there in an immersive experience', which in turn creates a 'transitional experience' as when 'the perception of the own body is pushed to the extreme, causing a most confusing corporal awareness' (Wynants et al., 2008: 161). A perfect virtual immersion, understood as an undisturbed illusion of being in a digitally produced space, does not offer the same kind of proprioceptive intensity as a more layered or interrupted immersion in which the participant is forced to negotiate and resolve a range of different and perhaps even contradictory stimuli in order to fully understand and appreciate their current location in the space. To capture the participant's experience in these more complex cases, Wynants et al. intro-duce the concept of 'synaesthetic negotiation' (italics removed), which they define as 'our tendency to unify the layered experience to a meaningful and coherent occurrence' and which, according to them, enables 'a heightened degree of presence' (Wynants et al., 2008: 160). They further explain this concept as our ability to relate, coordinate, and integrate different sensory inputs, and they directly link it with the 'transitional space':

> Although the senses are isolated and extended in the per-
> formance, spectators seem to be capable to unite the separate
> but simultaneous sensorial stimuli in a coherent and mean-
> ingful experience. Moreover, we seem to have the tendency

to adjust a small incongruence in the perceived stimuli. Relating these different impressions, sensorial stimuli and signs, one seems to integrate the different sensations in a seemingly coherent whole. In matching what we feel to what we see, the borders between different levels of reality are blurred. The immersant straddles between different medial worlds, which he experiences as one transitional world, in between different realities. (Wynants et al., 2008: 160)

The concept of 'synaesthetic negotiation' is thus fundamental for grasping the nature of the participant's experience in augmented and virtual reality.

In examining the sensory impact of extended reality performances, I therefore focus on the dramaturgical design of layered stimuli and environments, transitions between the environments, and the possibility of creating 'a transitional experience' through the process of 'synaesthetic negotiation'. Those elements of the performances are directly linked to Shakespeare's plays as inspirations. When pointing out the moments of sensory synaesthesia, I foreground the richness of sensory experience in the performance examples. According to Speicher et al. (2019: 3), mixed reality does not necessarily depend only on visual input; it can also involve auditory, kinaesthetic, haptic, gustatory, and olfactory stimuli. His observation also applies to the understanding of extended reality in this Element, and the sensory aspect is closely considered in the context of the adapted plays.

Another issue that is highlighted in this section concerns the ways in which physical and virtual environments are brought together for the effects of complementation and contrast, and to create the conditions for audience engagement. Chiel Kattenbelt, an academic and an associate dramaturg involved in CREW's extended reality project on *Hamlet*, underlined the importance of finding suitable dramaturgical frameworks that enable experiencers to effectively navigate the virtual environment and, if appropriate, to activate the virtual elements:

A virtual world can easily be constructed as a world in different dimensions or as a configuration of different worlds. For the dramaturgy of a virtual world, it is important to give the experiencer a clear idea of how the different spaces relate to each other and how the plurality of the space translates into clear instructions for navigation. Uncertainty about this immediately leads to passivity or causes the navigation to demand so much attention or to become such a challenge that there is hardly any space to take in all that is offered and especially to be discovered. With regard to the latter, it is very important to respect the experiencer's own agency. This assumes, insofar as controllers are used, that the experiencer has a clear idea of how to use them or even better to play with them. (Kattenbelt, 2021: 17)

Kattenbelt's observations point to the fundamental role of the experiencer in an extended reality performance, since in many cases the work might happen only if there is implicit or explicit interaction with the virtual elements. This occurs alongside social interaction with performers or other participants, given that extended reality theatre shares its fundamental characteristics with physical theatre as a communal space. What is more, there are particularly important parallels between extended reality theatre and Shakespeare's theatre, given that in the latter the presence of the audience and the communication between the actors and the spectators are not only essential but also explicit, considering the architecture of early modern playhouses and the broad range of metatheatrical strategies in the plays.

From this perspective, augmented and virtual reality in performance extend the strategies of metatheatre in that they enable the layering and interlacing of different orders of representation. In this context, metatheatre might be linked to Jay David Bolter and Richard Grusin's twin concepts of immediacy and hypermediacy, which are about the 'oscillation' between 'transparency and opacity', or, in other words, 'the promise' of 'a more immediate or authentic experience' that necessarily results in greater awareness of the nature of the medium (Bolter and Grusin, 2000: 19). This constant oscillation between being inside and outside the convention of a medium, and in particular the hypermediate act of drawing the user's attention to the framing of the medium, might be understood in extended reality performance as deeply metatheatrical if we define metatheatre as an act of self-referencing that balances between an impression of realism and the articulation of theatre as art. In extended reality theatre, such acts of oscillation or balancing encourage users to notice the means of making the work, but they also enable them to have a deeply intense experience of the medium. According to Wynants et al., '[e]xactly this tension – the negotiation between the real and the frame, between "looking through" and "looking at" – enhances "our sense of being there"' (Wynants et al., 2008: 162). Metatheatre might thus be further linked with the 'transitional experience' (Wynants et al., 2008: 161) as both depend on the processes of layering, negotiation, and reflection within the imagined world. Both are also able to make the user more aware of their experience and become more present.

The link between extended reality and metatheatre becomes particularly evident when we examine it through adaptations of Shakespeare's works, where elements of metatheatre encourage an exploration of immersive and interactive technologies. Lionel Abel, who coined the term 'metatheatre' in 1963, used Shakespeare's works as prime material for discussion, noting that the Elizabethan playwright 'experimented throughout his whole career with the play-within-a-play, sometimes introducing play-within-a-play sequences in his tragedies, almost always introducing such sequences in his comedies' (Abel, 1963: 66). Although in the examples mentioned here the engagement with the source varies from stagings of the whole script to acts of loose inspiration, all the works collected here demonstrate how Shakespeare's dramas can be used to advance our understanding of extended reality as a form of metatheatre.

Physical Space with Some Virtual Elements

In the first category of extended reality Shakespeare adaptations, audience members participate in a live performance that involves predominantly unmediated interaction with the actors in the shared space but also some moments of augmented and virtual reality. In such moments, the experiencers' perception of the physical environment can be extended or even entirely transformed through the inclusion of virtual elements, yet all the time they are grounded in the physical location, which remains the main locus of action. Introducing virtual elements into a live physical set-up calls for dramaturgical solutions that integrate digital devices in ways that are not gratuitous, impractical, or inadvertently confusing. In some cases, the experiencers might need help with accessing and operating the devices, but in every instance they will need an understanding of why such devices are introduced in the first place and, in particular, how their application might contribute to the interpretation of Shakespeare's dramas.

Examples of adaptations in this group include the RSC's *Tempest* (2016), CREW's *Hamlet's Lunacy* (2019), and Tim Crouch's *Truth's a Dog Must to Kennel* (2022). The RSC *Tempest*, a 135-minute-long live performance directed by Gregory Doran, featured an avatar of Ariel, played by motion-captured Mark Quartley, towering over the actors on stage. The spectators could simultaneously watch the live actor and his 3D imposing projection in an effect of augmented reality (yet without the need for a personal device). The use of an avatar was inspired by the themes of magic, spectacle, and metatheatre in Shakespeare's drama. Similarly, in CREW's *Hamlet's Lunacy*, an hour-long live performance in which the participants could experience moments of augmented and virtual reality through iPads and virtual reality headsets, the use of multiple environments was motivated by the themes of transition and crisis in *Hamlet* but also by the historical paradigm shift in Shakespeare's lifetime. Finally, in Crouch's *Truth's a Dog Must to Kennel*, a seventy-minute live performance, the experience of immersion was limited to a solo actor describing a staging of *King Lear* that he could have been seeing through a virtual reality headset. The audience could experience the immersion only vicariously, through the stories of the performer, who, in turn, was only imagining a virtual reality production. The performance presented theatre as an immersive and imaginative medium, in a nostalgic and bitter commentary on its demise, but also in reflection on madness and the ephemerality of life. In all three examples, Shakespeare's plays offered justification and inspiration for introducing virtual environments. In the following section, I focus on *Hamlet's Lunacy* as a production in which Shakespeare's source encouraged the artists to apply extended reality with a critical stance and in which experiencers could directly access augmented and virtual reality.

Hamlet's Lunacy

Hamlet's Lunacy was shown at KVS theatre in Brussels eight times from 10 to 13 April 2019, free of charge. It was co-directed by Eric Joris from the Brussels-based collective CREW, Mesut Arslan from the international network of artists Platform 0090, and Keez Duyves from the Amsterdam-based collective PIPS:lab. Kattenbelt, the professor of intermediality from Utrecht University, worked as a principal dramaturg on this production, while Jerry Killick, a regular collaborator of the British performance collective Forced Entertainment, contributed as a performer (Video 2).

The main artistic and organisational input for this production was provided by Joris and CREW. Established in 1991 by Joris, CREW has consistently experimented with cutting-edge technologies in live performance in collaboration with artists, academics, and scientists, including long-term partnership with the Expertise Centre for Digital Media at the University of Hasselt in Belgium. The company has applied tracking devices, virtual reality headsets, and visual displays in a number of performances in a range of

Video 2 *Hamlet's Lunacy* (2019). Courtesy of CREW. Video file available at http://www.cambridge.org/Mancewicz

innovative formats, such as arts installations, performance lectures, one-to-one shows, remote live theatre, and extended reality theatre. Research and conceptual exploration have been at the forefront of its work.

Since 2016, CREW has worked with academics, artists, and technicians on a practice-as-research project exploring *Hamlet* from the perspective of early modern history and science, which has resulted in a number of extended reality performances. Other collaborators on this project have included actors Thomas Dudkiewicz and Marijn Alexander de Jong from the Rotterdam-based collective URLAND, as well as academics Robin Nelson from the Royal Central School of Speech and Drama and Aneta Mancewicz. The guiding enquiry of the project was: How to act honourably in a conflicted world? The notion of the conflicted world referred to both the Renaissance period and the twenty-first century as two eras marked by dramatic paradigm shifts accompanied by a sense of uncertainty and insecurity. In its portrayal of early modern conflicts, CREW followed the idea that Shakespeare's tragedy expresses the major change in cultural imagery, science, society, and politics that occurred in sixteenth- and seventeenth-century England.

Several scholars have insisted on the notion of an early modern rupture. For instance, C. S. Lewis, in *Discarded Image: An Introduction to Medieval and Renaissance Literature*, claimed that the artists in the Middle Ages developed a discernible 'Model', that is, a collection of images and ideas that articulated their understanding of the universe, and that this Model was finally abandoned by the close of the seventeenth century (Lewis, 1964: 13). Similarly, Dan Falk argued that 'Shakespeare lived in a remarkable time' when '[t]he medieval world – a world of magic, astrology, witchcraft, and superstition of all kinds – was just beginning to give way to more modern ways of thinking', while 'new ideas about the human body, the Earth, and the universe at large were just starting to transform Western thought' (Falk, 2014: 6). According to Falk, traces of these 'new ideas' can be found in Shakespeare's plays, including *Hamlet* (Falk, 2014: 6–12, 145–69). Finally, the infamous Carl Schmitt observed that political intrigues concerning succession at the end of Queen Elizabeth's reign contributed to instability and unrest (Schmitt, 2006: 17). He also contended that between 1588 and 1688 England experienced a significant transition from barbarism to politics, or from feudalism to a modern state (Schmitt, 2006: 54–5), complemented by the move from land to sea and from links with Continental Europe to global imperialism (Schmitt, 2006: 55–6). Shakespeare's Globe as a popular playhouse in the capital benefitted from this transition since it was 'embedded in the creative, political, and economic fabric of early modern London, one of the leading centres of culture and commerce' (Mancewicz, 2018: 246). In 1600, around the time when Shakespeare wrote *Hamlet*, London became the headquarters of the East India Company, which in turn was an influential agent of imperialism and colonialism. Immensely powerful, the corporation was the owner of the *Red Dragon* ship, on whose board the tragedy was performed in 1607 off the west coast of Africa. In this first non-European performance of *Hamlet*, Shakespeare – an English playwright – became 'Shakespeare' – a global merchandise – while his work became forever inscribed in (post)colonial politics.

Thus, CREW's focus on a conflicted world in *Hamlet* points to striking parallels between Shakespeare's time and ours, but it also exposes cultural legacies of the early modern drive for global expansion. These parallels are not overt. As Kattenbelt explains: 'If we succeed in making perceivable and experienceable Hamlet's world as a world out of joint and in transition, then we have to trust the experiencer – and that means to take her/him seriously – that s/he is capable of making the connections with the lifeworld of today' (Kattenbelt, 2021: 34). At the same time, the broad political and cultural shifts that took place in the Renaissance were mapped in CREW's adaptation onto personal dilemmas, given that King James, Hamlet's alter ego in the production, struggled with the demands of revenge in the context of conflicting religious systems post-Reformation as well as competing legal frameworks. As Fredson Bowers (1940) and Roland Broude (1975) noted, the Renaissance period saw the transition from personal to public execution of revenge, with Hamlet being caught in between these two systems. By bringing up a range of such transitions, CREW adapted the source as a play about a protagonist troubled by the task of fixing a faulty system, in an echo of Hamlet's lines: 'The time is out of joint; O cursed spite/ That ever I was born to set it right!' (Shakespeare, 2007: 2.1.1.186–7). In an effort to allow the audience to embody the chaotic and changeable nature of the Renaissance period, CREW employed extended reality as a mode of engaging with the senses and perceptions of the experiencers.

In *Hamlet's Lunacy*, the notion of conflict and the ensuing sense of confusion were thus direct inspiration for the integration of augmented and virtual reality. During the performance, Killick interacted with a small group of experiencers in a spacious studio to explore themes from Shakespeare's tragedy. The script, co-written by Joris and Purni Morell, took a liberal approach to the source as it focused on Killick playfully addressing the participants. After initially introducing himself as Eric Joris (in Joris's presence), the actor went on to speak as King James, explaining the intricacies of the Renaissance reality, articulating analogies between himself and Hamlet, and supporting the experiencers with the use of digital devices in the production. His role as a guide was fundamental in establishing the conventions of this extended reality performance and providing a sense of live, physical interaction. Indeed, the performance featured direct exchanges with the audience, which included elements of improvisation. As an accomplished performer and a long-standing collaborator of Forced Entrainment, one of the most original performance collectives in the UK, Killick was well placed to improvise but also to perform King James and a few other characters playfully and self-reflexively.

Through the figure of King James, CREW's adaptation portrayed *Hamlet*'s historical contexts but also Hamlet as a thinking subject, as he was dealing with the transition from the medieval mindset to the modern one. To support the audience with understanding Hamlet's sense of uncertainty, doubt, and disorientation, CREW gave some participants direct access to augmented reality through hand-held iPads and to virtual reality through headsets and headphones, while others were invited to watch. In those instances, the perceptions of the immersants became altered, while their sense of space and their proprioception was disoriented. At the same time, throughout the piece, the audience participated in a live theatre experience. They were located in the same space, where they were guided by the physically present actor.

One of the key aspects of a conflicted world in *Hamlet's Lunacy* was the astronomical revolution in the sixteenth and seventeenth centuries. The debates about geocentric and heliocentric models were so important in Shakespeare's lifetime that the astronomer Peter Usher suggested reading *Hamlet* as 'an allegory about competing cosmological worldviews', in particular the theories of Ptolemy, Nicolaus Copernicus, and Tycho Brahe (cited in Falk, 2014: 10). The way that CREW interpreted the tragedy juxtaposed Ptolemaic and Tychonic models not only as scientific systems but also as distinctive worldviews with far-reaching religious and political implications, in accordance with the Renaissance tradition. Thus, the Ptolemaic system, with the stationary Earth placed at the centre, was linked to the Divine Order understood as the hierarchy of beings, with God and king at the top. Meanwhile, the Tychonic system, in which the stationary Earth is still at the centre, with the Sun and the Moon revolving around it, but with the planets orbiting the Sun, was associated in *Hamlet's Lunacy* with instability and disorder that might undermine the supreme status of God and king.

To enable the audience to embody the Ptolemaic model, CREW equipped several experiencers with iPads and encouraged them to move according to the path and the speed of their allocated planets, which they could see on the screens in an augmented reality mode (Figure 7). The scene was a modern recreation of human orreries. The enactment of orreries, that is, mechanical models of the solar system, was a common educational exercise in eighteenth-century English schools, and it continues in contemporary pedagogy and performance (Vanhoutte and Bigg, 2014: 259). In CREW's adaptation, the process was not entirely straightforward since the devices had to be calibrated, and the users had to adjust to them. This introduced moments of hesitation and confusion, in line with the dominant spirit of this adaptation. By using augmented reality, CREW enhanced the experience of the audience members and strengthened their sense of presence. The iPad users were invited to combine the kinaesthetic stimuli with the visual ones; they had to bring together physical and virtual worlds in the act of 'synaesthetic negotiation' (Wynants et al., 2008: 160). In this way, they were given the opportunity to personally experience the Ptolemaic model, while the spectators watching this process were able to see it working in practice. The application of augmented reality transformed the appearance of the physical space, but it also turned the experiencers accessing this technology into a spectacle.

Perhaps the most important scene in terms of extended reality exploration occurred, however, at the end of the performance, when the physical

Figure 7 *Hamlet's Lunacy* (2019). Courtesy of CREW.

and the virtual elements were enmeshed through the combination of imagery, music, and movement. It began with a projection on two large screens, which were attached to computers and placed on movable stands. A castle, a map, and avatars of Shakespeare's characters, artfully redrawn by Joris, who has extensive experience in comics design, emerged in quick succession on the screens only to immediately disintegrate, decay, and disappear. Meanwhile, poignant music composed by Christoph De Boeck filled the room. Some of the audience members were wearing virtual reality headsets and headphones, while holding onto the stick attached to the stand. This allowed them to become fully immersed in the projections and the music. Soon the stage hands began to move the stands, first slowly, then faster and faster, so that the immersants were eventually forced to run. Finally, the stands were placed opposite each other. For a while, they were rotating in the space until they gradually came to a standstill. Then the projections and the music stopped. This marked the end of the performance.

In this scene, the immersants and the screens became part of the performance design and dramaturgy. Occupying the whole space of the studio, they created a hybrid choreography of physical bodies and digital images. The final sequence recreated the pathos of *Hamlet*'s tragic ending. It captured the play's fragility, ephemerality, and mortality through the combination of visual, aural, and kinaesthetic stimuli. The immersants had the possibility to experience the sense of finality and sorrow that defines the unhappy conclusion of Shakespeare's drama through what Nelson describes as 'a dizzying virtual environment of shifting geo-spatial imagery' (Nelson, 2022: 90). Running through the space, immersed in the poignant music soundtrack and the captivating images of destruction, the participants could sense the sadness of this tragedy without recourse to lines from the play, in a way that was indescribably intense because it was embodied. For those accessing the scene through virtual reality headsets, this final run offered an exceptional opportunity to inhabit *Hamlet* as a complex of emotions and ideas. The immersants did not become one of the characters, nor did they enter a scene enacted by the actors/avatars to watch it as a close witness. Instead, they became present in a poetic world of collages and transitions to the point of embodying and feeling it. This allowed them to access *Hamlet*'s dominant mood of death and decay through their own senses and emotions.

What was central in this scene was the complex combination of physical and virtual stimuli, which oscillated between complementation and contrast. The experiences were immersed in the virtual reality, but they were also subject to physical demands and constraints. Running with the headset while being attached to the screen required stamina and responsiveness, and it enhanced corporeal awareness. It forced the experiencers to integrate the sensory input from the physical and virtual environments, while being fully present in both of them. They had to coordinate the tactile stimuli with the virtual images seen through the headset and the mediated sound through the headphones to have a coherent perception of the hybrid space.

This resulted in a unique kind of 'transitional experience' (Wynants et al., 2008: 161) that was about being in the extended reality space not in the form of either/or but rather in the form of both/and. In principle (though not in the exact configuration of technologies and stimuli), this performance strategy was similar to what CREW achieved in the production of *EUX* performed at La Chartreuse (Centre national des écritures du spectacle – the National Playwriting Centre) in Villeneuve-les-Avignon, France, in 2008. As Wynants et al. describe *EUX*: 'The correlation between different sensorial stimuli, meaning the coherence between for example the mediated image seen through the goggles and the live tactile sensations and/or the sound is introduced as an immersive strategy to blur the boundaries between live and mediated and creating thus a strong feeling of being physically present in this mixed reality' (Wynants et al., 2008: 160). While both these productions questioned the boundaries of perception and knowledge, their ultimate goal was to allow the experiencers to have an intense sense of presence and embodiment.

The focus of *Hamlet's Lunacy* was thus not on representing the plot but on using visual, aural, and kinaesthetic stimuli to enable the experiencers to embody it. Augmented and virtual reality devices were crucial means to this end, and their application was directly inspired by CREW's interpretation of the tragedy. Focusing on the Renaissance paradigm shift and Hamlet's struggle to understand the rapidly changing reality, the company sought to give the audience members the possibility of experiencing the protagonist's disorientation by expanding and altering their perceptions. In CREW's adaptation, Hamlet's confusion and madness found their expression outside language, so that the protagonist's emotion became embodied by the participants. This became particularly evident in the final scene, which allowed the selected audience members to experience the sense of turmoil and frenzy as they were rushed through the space while being immersed in monumental music and images.

At the same time, the production was a work in progress, with dramaturgy in development and occasional issues with data transfer. While the guide was helpful in facilitating the transitions between different themes, characters, and technological devices, he was also tasked with introducing a broad array of historical contexts, so at times the participants might have felt overwhelmed. Given that extended reality requires a heightened level of attention from the users, who need to become accustomed to augmented and virtual reality both operationally and experientially, introducing elaborate plotlines and situations is risky. *Hamlet's Lunacy* would have benefitted from greater selectivity and a narrower focus on Renaissance ideas to allow for more emphasis on perception and embodiment. This would have made it easier for the participants to engage with Shakespeare's tragedy on a sensory rather than a cerebral level. Such engagement, in turn, might have more clearly foregrounded the feeling of mutability, mortality and evanescence. This would have enabled the experiencers to grasp intuitively the primordial and polyphonic nature of death, which is the basis of *Hamlet* and indeed any tragedy that explicitly explores the fragility of life. Still, CREW and its collaborators were able to offer some of this intuition to the experiencers in the final sequence with the moving screens. They also managed to show how augmented and virtual reality could be integrated into the interpretation of the source to bring the participants closer to *Hamlet* as a tragedy of a conflicted individual in a conflicted time.

Physical and Virtual Spaces Balanced

In the second category, physical and virtual spaces are more or less equally interwoven in the performance. This might involve either complementation of the spaces, as in the case of Nexus's *Tempest*, a ten-minute augmented reality experience in the experiencers' homes, or the spaces being on the continuum, as in the case of the Royal Opera House's

Current, Rising (2021), a fifteen-minute hyper-reality opera that was as a fully immersive virtual performance located within a carefully curated physical set-up. Finally, in Krzysztof Garbaczewski's two-hour-long production of *Midsummer Night's Dream* at Narodowy Teatr Stary (the National Stary Theatre) in Kraków (2022), the physical and the virtual spaces ran parallel to each other. When the actors in virtual reality headsets entered the world of sexual desires and psychedelic fantasies, the audience watched the virtual environment as projections on screen. In each case, the physical and the virtual spaces were closely connected to extend the sensorium of the experiencers.

The dramaturgical challenge of these set-ups consisted in ensuring that throughout the performance the physical and virtual spaces were meaningfully linked to each other but also to the source text. In all three cases, Shakespeare's plays provided direct stimulus for the use of digital devices, encouraging the inclusion of poetry, music, and metatheatre as an inspiration for an alternative performance dramaturgy. In exploring sociability and solitude through the use of extended reality, Nexus's *Tempest* and the Royal Opera House's *Current, Rising* were inspired by Shakespeare's portrayal of isolated individuals on a magical island. In Garbaczewski's *Midsummer Night's Dream*, in turn, virtual reality became the locus of wild imagination. Its inclusion within a shared theatrical space, where the audience could see both the actors on stage and their avatars on screen, allowed the spectators to reflect on the strategies and constraints of acting in an immersive environment but also on the implications of applying virtual reality to stage Shakespeare's comedy. In the subsequent section, I offer an analysis of *Current, Rising* as an example of a multisensory experience in which both physical and virtual spaces have been carefully crafted and curated.

Current, Rising (2021)

Current, Rising was shown at the Royal Opera House from 21 May to 10 June 2021, after the planned premiere on 19 December 2020 had to be cancelled owing to Covid-19 restrictions. The full-priced tickets cost £20. The production was directed by Netia Jones, designed by Joanna Scotcher, and written by Melanie Wilson. Similarly to *Hamlet's Lunacy* and *Dream*, the piece emerged from a long period of collaborative practice that involved high-profile partners such as the Royal Opera House; Figment Productions, a digital media production company; and StoryFutures, a £12 million research centre based at Royal Holloway, University of London, that focuses on immersive storytelling and that, like the RSC *Dream*, is funded by UK Research and Innovation's Audience of the Future programme. Developed through interdisciplinary collaboration and supported with research funding, the production was an experiment that aimed to explore the intersection of virtual reality and opera. (Here is the link to the work: www.youtube.com/watch?v= eY0GioXHBL4.)

Current, Rising allowed the participants to access the physical and the virtual as complementary categories on the continuum. Designed as an intimate experience for four people at a time, accompanied by a guide, the performance took place at the Linbury theatre, inside an illuminated wooden box structure with the large sign 'Current, Rising' on the walls. The guides in this production were not explicitly embedded in the plot; their role was more technical and supportive, in comparison to *Hamlet's Lunacy*. Still, they were indispensable, providing a vital assistance to the participants in the passage from the physical to the virtual environment. As the experiencers entered the box, they could read a curated statement about the aims of the piece, which focused on the universal themes of separation and communication. The statement also emphasised the connection with *The Tempest* as the source and articulated the key question of *Current, Rising*, which strongly resonated with the period of the Covid-19 pandemic: 'What do we build from here?'

The sleek box set, with white walls covered with black letters, became the setting for the virtual reality immersion. As the participants adjusted the headsets, they could see the walls and the ceiling turn grey, while the low sound playing in the theatre was replaced by different voices reciting Ariel's song 'Full fathom five' from *The Tempest* (Shakespeare 1999, 1.2.397–403). Meanwhile, the fellow experiencers were transformed into avatars visible in the space as companions in the journey. In this brief moment, the participants had a particularly powerful 'transitional experience' in which the physical and the virtual environments overlapped, allowing the immersants to have an intense experience of the space as a palimpsest. As the physical space was being overwritten by a virtual one, the users were forced to adjust their perception in order to integrate the physical and the virtual input. The moment was followed by a series of explorations in virtual environments, where a range of stimuli affected the participants' proprioception and forced them to perform what Wynants et al. (2008: 160) define as 'synaesthetic negotiation'. The performance finished with the users coming back together as avatars into the initial space with white walls and black letters. The final virtual image consisted of the words 'Current, Rising' on the black surface, as a reference to the title displayed on the wooden box at the Linbury theatre. After the experiencers removed the headsets, they were invited to read the libretto and the production credits displayed on the walls of the set.

The seamless transitions between the physical and the virtual sets made it possible for the participants to see the two as part of the same reality, situated on the spectrum, with the experiencers inside the work. The wooden box at the Linbury theatre thus functioned not only as a stage for the immersion but also as a portal to the virtual world, since the experiencers were invited to walk through a virtual door leading them to other digital environments. At the same time, by opening and closing the virtual journey with images of the physical set, Jones aimed to blur the boundary between actuality and imagination, inviting the participants to witness the transformation of their surroundings and the dissolution of the laws of physics. Moreover, and perhaps most importantly, in suspending the laws of physics and situating the experiencers on the physical–virtual continuum, the director aimed to create a space in which they could become not only observers but also makers of their own experience. She believed that this opportunity was particularly valuable for opera as a medium, which has historically been hierarchical and exclusive. As Jones explained (cited in Oliver, 2020):

> With *Current, Rising*, we have been exploring the possibilities
> of VR to expand the idea of what an opera can be, both in the
> process of creation, and in the audience experience. VR chal-
> lenges all the traditional hierarchies of opera and classical music,
> and allows a completely different approach. It is the most
> democratic of all media – it can subvert the laws of physics

> so why would it need to conform to the usual rules of cultural exchange? It provides a space where music, the visual world and the physical experience are completely enmeshed, changing the relationships between the creators, the usual sequence of creation, and the relationship of the audience to the work. Here the audience are the protagonists, they are inside the work, and their physical experience is a part of the work itself.

Even if the notion of virtual reality as 'the most democratic of all media' might need to be taken with a grain of salt (after all, access to the medium requires a relatively expensive headset), it is easy to see how Jones has successfully exploited the medium's interactive and participatory nature. Experiencers were invited inside – inside the wooden box and inside the virtual world – where they could move around and explore the space. During select moments, they could also manipulate and transform the virtual environment through movement. As such, they were given some degree of agency and the sense of being a group of equals, where everyone had the same opportunity to get a close and unobstructed view of the performance, without distinctions based on ticket prices. Such an equitable experience was of course possible thanks to research and development funding. As the anonymous *Salterton Arts Review* contributor sensibly noted about *Current, Rising*, '[i]t must be expensive to run by the time you've developed it, kitted it out, and taken over a performance space for something only a handful of people can do at once. But in that sense this is the perfect time to do it – you can't have that many people together anyway so why not push the boundaries?' (Anonymous, 2021). The period of the Covid-19 pandemic thus provided a good opportunity to explore more intimate formats of performance in virtual reality, but the question remains how those formats can be continued beyond that period and how they can be economically viable for artists with little or no access to public funding.

In *Current, Rising*, public funding made it possible for the creative team to develop a technologically complex work that activated several senses of the participants through a breathtaking design. The main input was provided by high-quality visuals, which resulted in stunning effects. The immersion offered several spatial configurations through the imagery of

Figure 8 *Current, Rising* (2021). Courtesy of Joanna Scotcher.

gigantic staircases, elevated platforms, and an immense sea landscape (Figure 8).

These virtual worlds enabled the participants to have the feeling of being lifted up and of drifting in the air or being at sea. According to Alexandra Coghlan, this gave the experiencers a dizzying and disorienting experience comparable to 'a theme-park': 'You marvel, flinch and gasp at the effects – an Escher-like universe of impossible architecture, buildings swallowed up by ground that rumbles and shakes beneath your feet, wind off the ocean whipping round your face, a horizon that dances and pulses with light' (Coghlan, 2021). When I experienced the performance, my proprioception was heightened in those moments. While I felt suspended on a platform among the staircases, or while I was looking up and having an almost suffocating feeling of being underwater, I had to reassure myself of my centre of gravity, my position in the space, and my safety.

These impressions felt even more real because of the variety of other inputs, such as the wind blowing on the experiencers at key moments, giving them the impression of being suspended in the space. As Jochan Embley put it, '[i]t doesn't stop with the visuals either. At some points, a breeze wraps around me and the floor begins to shake' (Embley, 2021).

Simon Reveley, chief executive officer of Figment Productions, explained that his company created a range of sensory effects as part of 'a "hyper reality" platform' with an aim 'to enable a group of people to move freely around a virtual world in a shared space, seeing each other as avatars and exploring a world that features real world effects like wind, rumble, movement and tactile objects' (cited in Oliver, 2020). The participants thus encountered a combination of sensory stimuli of virtual and natural origin that they had to integrate to create a coherent experience through the process of 'synaesthetic negotiation' (Wynants et al., 2008: 160). As the virtual environments changed from a vertical image of the staircases to a horizontal image of the sea, the experiencers had to rapidly adjust their perception of space. For instance, in the scene with the sea, they were invited to relate the virtual image in the headset to the effect of the wind. The coordination of different stimuli was central to ensuring that in each instance the users had a strong sense of immersion and presence.

The large-scale visual elements were further complemented in the performance by monumental opera music and singing, which involved Samantha Fernando's compositions, Anna Dennis's soprano, and CHROMA ensemble's performance. However, according to George Hall, the musical elements were overshadowed by the visual input: 'Despite the haunting singing of soprano Anna Dennis, Fernando's atmospheric score is more background than foreground: the journey on which one travels is primarily visual' (Hall, 2021). Similarly, Embley admitted with a hint of guilt that '[w]ith all this happening, I realise that I'm not paying as much attention to the audio as I should be' (Embley, 2021). Coghlan (2021) also noted that, because proprioception was at the forefront of the immersion, it was difficult to listen to and understand the libretto. I was also focused predominantly on the visuals and the movement in the space; only at some points could I make explicit connections between the images and the words.

This ultimately brings me to the question of the role of Shakespeare's drama as a source for this production. *Current, Rising* was marketed as '[i]nspired by the liberation of Ariel at the end of Shakespeare's *The Tempest*' (Oliver, 2020). However, the libretto was difficult to follow: either it was delivered by a multiplicity of voices or it was sung operatically; most importantly, it was drowned by the dominant presence of the visual stimuli affecting the immersants' proprioception. As Ivan Hewett observed, '[t]he libretto and poems are hard to hear; the musical score by Samantha Dickinson is plaintive but hardly distinctive', while 'most of one's attention is taken up by thinking "don't be scared, that's not a real precipice you're looking down on"' (Hewett, 2021). The dominance of the visual material and the difficulty in understanding the text might explain why Coghlan noted that for her the performance felt 'fundamentally like a vehicle for technology' (Coghlan, 2021). The sensory surplus of virtual reality combined with the complexity of Shakespeare's poetry (rendered even more opaque by the use of opera) resulted in an experience that might have felt confusing and disorienting at times. Moreover, the inclusion of Shakespeare's lines did not provide a particularly relevant link to the source. A much more powerful inspiration from *The Tempest* came in the form of dramaturgy.

Current, Rising was structured as a progression of episodes, explorations, and parallels. Coghlan's description of the dramaturgical format foregrounds an open approach that reveals an intriguing connection between the source and the adaptation: 'A concept – a newly freed Ariel at the end of *The Tempest* travels through worlds and times, urging us, the earthbound audience, to join him – provides the loosest of dramatic structures, a platform for a sequence of visual and physical sensations, digital "rooms", each with their own distinct character' (Coghlan, 2021). Shakespeare's inspiration in this case might have consisted precisely in providing an episodic dramaturgical model, as in his drama multiple groups are skilfully orchestrated during their stay on the island. In recognition of this composite structure, Jan Kott (1967) famously saw *The Tempest*, and other Shakespeare plays, as a series of repeated scenarios that would allow the audience to experience the same situation from different perspectives and in distinctive genre conventions. He argued that the Elizabethan playwright did not design his works 'on the principle of unity of action, but on the principle of analogy, comprising a double, treble, or quadruple plot, which repeats the same basic theme; they are a system of mirrors, as it were, both concave and convex, which reflect, magnify and parody the same situation' (Kott, 1967: 245). Seen in this light, Shakespeare's dramaturgy provides a useful framework for exploration of the participants' perceptions through a range of interconnected sensory set-ups in *Current, Rising*.

What perhaps was missing from this exploration was a chance for the experiencers to see the seams between the physical and the virtual environments. Strategically located moments of rupture in the fabric of immersion and illusion could have foregrounded virtual reality as a medium and shown its hypermediacy. As the anonymous contributor to the *Salterton Arts Review* rightly observes, in *Current, Rising* 'you never see "behind the curtain" so to speak. The spell remains unbroken' (Anonymous, 2021). The chance to see the skill behind the spell would have established more explicitly the links with *The Tempest* as a self-reflexive, metatheatrical play. It would have allowed the participants to experience more fully Ariel's mischievous and creative spirit, as well as Shakespeare's fascination with art and appearance.

With the opening storm, which merges realism, magic, and theatricality, Shakespeare inscribes his drama in the framework of metatheatre and hypermediacy. As I wrote elsewhere, '*The Tempest* has an extraordinary potential to play with the audience's imagination – it invites us to enter a magical world in one instance, only to reveal its fictionality in the next one' (Mancewicz, 2023: 102). The drama, therefore, lends itself particularly well to explorations of not only theatre as a medium but also the nature of representation and imagination more broadly. It is an ideal text to which to apply 'the logic of hypermediacy' in which 'the artist (or multimedia programmer or web designer) strives to make the viewer acknowledge the medium as a medium and to delight in that acknowledgment' (Bolter and Grusin, 2000: 41–2). Shakespeare's dramaturgy of analogous scenarios is particularly relevant here, given that Bolter and Grusin describe the operation of hypermediacy precisely as the process of 'multiplying spaces and media and . . . repeatedly redefining the visual and conceptual relationships among mediated spaces – relationships that may range from simple juxtaposition to complete absorption' (Bolter and Grusin, 2000: 42). There seem to be some productive overlaps between mirroring a theme in a range of situations and styles in Shakespeare's dramas and creating multiple environments that foreground different characteristics of the media in extended reality. Perhaps these overlaps might have been explored more explicitly in the production.

Although *Current, Rising* successfully employed the strategy of spatial multiplication, there could have been more range in terms of creating the relationships between the spaces and the media in the production. For instance, the physical and the virtual sets might have been positioned more clearly alongside each other in ways that would have allowed the experiencers to grasp the layered nature of this performance and to perceive virtual reality as a frame or an interface. Such insight would have brought the participants closer to the core of Shakespeare's play and allowed them to experience more fully the hybrid nature of extended reality. At the same time, *Current, Rising* was effective in providing participants with a 'transitional experience' in which they were invited to synchronise the natural and the virtual stimuli in the process of 'synaesthetic negotiation'. This ensured a highly engaging experience for the users.

Virtual Space with Some Physical Elements

The third category discussed in this section focuses on performances that take place in the virtual environment, with some physical elements supporting the experience of the participants to a varying degree. One example is *To Be With Hamlet*, by David Gochfeld and Javier Molina, developed in collaboration with New York University Tandon School of Engineering, which premiered in 2017 at the Tribeca Film Festival. Similarly to *Current, Rising*, the production involved multi-user virtual reality technology to allow the experiencers to see each other as avatars, as they were all part of the immersion in real time. Another example in this category is Tender Claws' *Tempest*, a forty-minute live interactive show in the virtual space that was available online from 9 July to 30 September 2020, and then again in March 2021. Finally, in the RSC's *Dream*, a thirty-minute experience streamed in March 2021, the audience watched the actors performing in the virtual environment but also acting in a physical studio.

The three performances took place entirely online, yet in all of them the participants and the actors were embedded in the work to some degree. Even though the productions adapted very different Shakespeare's dramas – *Hamlet*, *The Tempest*, and *A Midsummer Night's Dream*, respectively – they all foregrounded magical and supernatural themes from the sources, while aiming to foster a strong sense of connection between the immersants and the performers, on the one hand, and among the immersants themselves, on the other. The analysis that follows focuses on *Dream* because of the production's explicit emphasis on its hybrid status.

Dream by the RSC (2021)

Dream was shown online from 12 to 20 March 2021 with ten performances scheduled at different times of the day to accommodate audiences across the globe. The show was adapted into a remotely accessible experience during the UK national lockdown, after a live immersive performance planned for June 2020 had to be cancelled. The performance was available for free, yet with the possibility of purchasing Audience Plus tickets for £10, which allowed holders to interact with the virtual environment using the touchscreen, trackpad, or mouse on their devices. The ticket marketing website and the virtual lobby provided access to the performance and introduced the audience to the design and atmosphere of the piece. One could watch *Dream* on a computer, a phone, or a tablet with fairly low-tech specification, while the heavy lifting of the visual and sound design was achieved through a process of expensive and elaborate collaboration among the RSC, the Manchester International Festival (MIF), Marshmallow Laser Feast (MLF), and the Philharmonia Orchestra. The production was funded as one of four Audience of the Future Demonstrator projects within the Audience of the Future consortium, which involved collaboration with partners such as Goldsmiths University, London and NESTA. The research focus was on audience participation and the financial viability of such work. A recording of the production was available online until 30 September 2021, but it did not attract the same level of attention as the real-time performances in March (Video 3).

The production was directed by Robin McNicholas, founder and creative director of the immersive art collective Marshmallow Laser Feast, with the narrative developed by McNicholas and Pippa Hill, Head of Literary at the RSC. Hill was also responsible for writing the script, which drew on selected lines, ideas, and structural devices from *A Midsummer Night's Dream*. The adaptation was marketed as 'inspired by the themes of'

Video 3 *Dream* (2021). Courtesy of the Royal Shakespeare Company, in collaboration with the Manchester International Festival, Marshmallow Laser Feast, and the Philharmonia Orchestra. Video file available at http://www.cambridge.org/Mancewicz

Shakespeare's comedy (RSC, 2021a), with Sarah Ellis, the RSC director of digital development, explaining that '[i]t's not a performance of the play, but it's inspired by the world of the play and the themes of the play' (RSC, 2021a). As in most extended reality adaptations of Shakespeare, the narrative was simple, with no complex plot development but instead a classic story arc, involving build-up, climax, and resolution. In *Dream*, the experiencers, guided by Puck (played by EM Williams), entered and explored the forest to find the fairies, then saw the destruction of the natural habitat, and, finally, witnessed its regeneration. At the same time, a simple story does not necessarily mean that a production cannot tackle important social themes. *Dream* and *Current, Rising* more or less overtly addressed the climate crisis, whereas *Hamlet's Lunacy* foregrounded a scientific and political revolution. Ormerod generously summarised *Dream* thus: 'The story is slight, to say the least, but there is just enough of one, and there is genuine drama and wonder here' (Ormerod, 2021). In keeping with the notion of 'wonder', the narrative arc in the production was supported mainly by richly layered imagery and music, which resulted in a deeply engaging journey for the audience, one in which Shakespeare's poetry was turned into a visual and musical exploration.

To design *Dream*, the creative team chose Unreal Engine, a 3D computer graphics creation tool that the RSC had already applied in its live-theatre performance of *The Tempest* in 2016 to develop and animate the avatar of Ariel on stage. Created by Epic Games, an American video game and software developer, Unreal Engine has been used for the real-time 3D design of video games, including Fortnite, as well as films and television series such as the American space western *The Mandalorian* (2019–). In *Dream*, Unreal Engine allowed the team to build evocative environments and backgrounds where avatars of the performers interacted in the virtual space thanks to computer software and forty-eight motion-capture cameras. The application of an advanced graphics software enabled sophisticated play with scale, depth, distance, perspective, and movement, particularly in the sequences of flying, moving across and above the trees, or in a scene with Puck shrinking to enter a hollow. There was also visual layering, as in the image of a spider walking in the foreground, with Puck appearing behind, which contributed to an effect of depth in the image on the screen.

The 3D graphics generated in this piece were of such high quality that Hilary Lamb described them as 'competitive with the current generation of video games' (Lamb, 2021). They were also slightly surreal, with leaves as dots and with the characters as imaginary creatures representing different forms of nature. Each fairy had a distinctive identity inspired by the natural world: Puck was a collection of rocks, Peaseblossom (Jamie Morgan) an assortment of twigs, Moth (Durassie Kiangangu) a mass of small moths in the shape of a moth, Mustardseed (Loren O'Dair) a face formed of roots, and Cobweb (Maggie Bain) a gigantic eye covered with webs. Using nature-inspired avatars required a novel acting approach from the performers, who were successfully supported by the movement director Sarah Perry. It also made it possible to avoid assigning gender roles to the avatars, which worked well in the portrayal of supernatural, boundary-crossing fairies from Shakespeare's *Midsummer Night's Dream*. Williams, a non-binary performer who opened the show wearing a shirt with the sign 'they/them', noted about their part that '[i]t's a non gender-specific role and there's this fizziness of adolescence about Puck' (cited in Sutherland, 2021). A similarly fluid approach to gender was used in Nexus's *Tempest*, which was gender-blind, with avatars designed to represent different elements, in accordance with Shakespeare's exploration of nature in the source drama. In this sense, extended reality has an exciting potential to open up different gender fluidities as a way not only of exploring Shakespeare's complex characterisation but also of encouraging more inclusive casting practices.

In *Dream*, the portrayal of the fairies as part of the natural world was directly connected with the poetic, shimmering language of its source. Hill insisted on being faithful to Shakespeare's script: 'I went through the play and found every mention of a plant, a flower, a tree or a creature that appears in that wood and the list has been given to the Visual Developers to work with' (RSC, 2021b). Shakespeare's text was thus translated into poetic visuals, as in the case of a decrepit castle in CREW's *Hamlet's Lunacy*, the vertiginous landscapes of *Current, Rising*, the luscious nature in Nexus's *Tempest*, or the bold and simple imagery of Tender Claws' *Tempest*. In all these examples, the aim was not to realistically represent the world but to introduce an imaginative space that would allow the experiencers to explore their embodiment and proprioception.

At the same time, typically for extended reality productions, visuals were inherently linked with music to build the dramaturgy of the piece and enable the experience of immersion on a flat screen. In *Dream*, this included classical music and two contemporary orchestral pieces: excerpts from Esa-Pekka Salonen's *Gemini* and Jesper Nordin's *Ärr*. The music was recorded with the participation of 100 musicians from the Philharmonia Orchestra, conducted by Salonen, the orchestra's principal conductor and artistic advisor, on 13 March 2020, right before the UK lockdown. The pre-recorded music was combined in performance with the soundscape created by the audio director Anastasia Devane, who was responsible for such sounds as the blowing of the wind, and the cracking of the twigs that accompanied Puck's movement. Finally, Nordin as interactivity designer and creative adviser for this production introduced an interactive music device, Gestrument, which allowed the performers to generate music with their movements in real time yet in harmony with the pre-recorded orchestral score.

Gestrument was one of the interactive tools employed in this piece, enabling the performers to make an impact on the virtual world through their movement, which was directly translated into sound. Another tool was given to Audience Plus spectators, who were invited to launch fireflies and plant seeds during the performance. In the run-up to the production, the possibility of audience interaction was strongly endorsed by the makers and the producers of *Dream*. As Ellis announced, '[w]e are using the latest gaming technology, live broadcast techniques, and performance technology to enable the actors and audience to interact with each other in real-time' (RSC, 2021a). In practice, however, the interaction turned out be rather underwhelming, with several reviewers complaining that it was impossible to see what each Audience Plus spectator actually contributed, given the vast number of participants engaged in the process. The disappointment was particularly acute given the high expectations concerning this production, which were fuelled not only by press releases but also by the show's reliance on a popular computer engine, which might have suggested to the users that there would be more opportunities to play. Lamb (2021) and Peter Kirwan (2021) explicitly complained that it was frustrating to watch the show, as if one were witnessing someone else play a computer game. This suggests that video-game design might be problematic in extended reality performances as it could encourage users to expect a fully interactive and immersive experience. What theatre-makers might want to explore instead is the contrast between the immediacy and the hypermediacy of virtual reality. The aim in this case would be *not* to fully immerse the audience members in a virtual environment but to provide them with a 'transitional experience' (Wynants et al., 2008: 160) in which they could engage with physical and virtual environments as both complementary and contrasting worlds.

In *Dream*, the shifts between physical and virtual spaces punctuated the dramaturgy of performance, occupying prominent positions in the structure of the piece: the opening, the climax, and the conclusion. The show began in the lobby of Portsmouth Guildhall, with Williams in a motion-capture suit speaking to the camera to introduce themselves as Puck and inviting the audience to follow them down a corridor of Portsmouth Guildhall to the studio. Similarly, *Hamlet's Lunacy* started with Killick outside the studio of KVS theatre, addressing the spectators and leading them inside the performance space, whereas *Current, Rising* featured a guide welcoming the participants. The striking similarity between these productions suggests the importance of the guide figure in extended reality theatre as someone who can establish direct connection with the audience, facilitate the use of technology, and contribute to the experience of liveness in the show. The presence of a live guide might also be a way of grounding the performance in the physical space. This was particularly important in *Dream* as an online show, in which, after the brief introduction, the audience joined the virtual world of the forest, this time led by Williams as an avatar. From that moment, the experiencers were immersed in the digital imagery and music, following Puck on a quest to find the fairies and save the forest from a catastrophic storm.

In the climax of the production, which saw the obliteration of the environment and the fairies, the camera zoomed out to reveal the studio with Williams and the other performers in motion-capture suits. The audience could see the actors animating the avatars against a large projection screen, which showed the virtual reality world with a slightly pixelated texture. The set-up encouraged the viewers to compare the gestures of the performers with the virtual representations of their avatars. In this scene the virtual and the physical spaces were set side by side to foreground the performance as a process and a product, creating an effect of hypermediacy (Figure 9).

Similarly, in CREW's virtual reality installation *Hands-on-Hamlet* (2017), the immersants could access two kinds of environment: 3D graphics of a dilapidated castle with avatars of Shakespeare's characters and 360-degree video footage from rehearsals with actors in motion-capture suits recording the performances. The experiencers could freely switch between these two environments by putting their heads into a spherical shape inside the virtual reality installation. As such, they could play with different kinds of representation and reality.

In *Dream*, the studio scenes at the beginning and in the middle of the performance also provided the participants with an opportunity to compare parallel realities, but they were crucial for other reasons too. According to Benjamin Broadribb, they offered much-needed legitimacy to the work of the performers, particularly in the period of the pandemic: 'With opportunities to see actors perform live in the same space as each other so much rarer in the

Figure 9 *Dream* (2021). Photo by Stuart Martin.

preceding year, showing the human beings behind the avatars, both in these opening moments and later on, gave *Dream* a sense of tangibility and authenticity it might otherwise have lacked' (Broadribb, 2021: 493). At the same time, the climax scene was profoundly metatheatrical, with the disruption of immersion leading to the effects of doubling and hypermediacy. Broadribb perceptively noted how the use of metatheatre was aligned in this instance with the role of the mechanicals in *A Midsummer Night's Dream*: 'The VR performance was repositioned as a performance-within-the-performance. As Williams cried out "Help me, for I am weary", they were both the supernatural sprite within the forest realm and the actor performing in isolation a year into the pandemic' (Broadribb, 2021: 494). In addition, the production introduced a specific reference to the performance of the mechanicals. Broadribb argues that when Williams as an actor and a character said, 'Sweet friends, I thank thee for thy sunny beams, for thy gracious golden glittering gleams', their words adapted Bottom's lines from the *Pyramus and Thisbe* performance in *A Midsummer Night's Dream* (Shakespeare, 2017: 5.1.265, 267) and 'deftly drew a sincere parallel between the live performers and the mechanicals' (Broadribb, 2021: 494). In an ironic twist, when the RSC performer seemed to be speaking sincerely to the viewers, their words were taken directly from an actor's speech in Shakespeare's drama. Thus, Williams' double presence (as a motioned-captured body and its virtual representation) not only allowed the audience to see the physical and the virtual environments as parallel and complementary realities but also introduced a complex combination of authenticity and acting.

By showing the effects of motion capture in this scene of *Dream*, and also by revealing how these effects are made, the performance did not strive to offer the audience an uninterrupted immersion. Instead, the production aimed to give them an understanding that what they were witnessing was an act of make-believe. It was highly poignant that such metatheatrical awareness coincided in *Dream* with the portrayal of ecological catastrophe, which might have suggested that moments of crisis can create opportunities for reflection and change. Once the crisis was mitigated, the performance moved back to the immersive mode in which the audience could witness the revival of the fairies and the forest. *Dream* concluded with a curtain call, which again revealed the actors in motion-capture suits, who then participated in a post-show discussion with the cast and the creatives that involved live questions from the audience. The discussion was an important reminder about the real-time dimension of the performance, but it was also a chance for the spectators to interact and engage, which was particularly meaningful in the lockdown period.

Although the RSC *Dream* was an online production, it involved an interplay of physical and virtual spaces in which Shakespeare's language was translated into visual and musical design that aimed to activate the senses of the experiencers. Matt Wolf was attentive to this translation in portraying the performance's effect as 'a sensory feast that aims to find a visual correlative for one strand of an infinitely elastic play whose woodlands can be a place of release and ecstasy, on the one hand, foreboding and danger on the other' (Wolf, 2022). At the same time, *Dream*'s preoccupation with the senses was deeply self-reflexive and metatheatrical. This might have led

Sarah Hemming to describe this production as 'a 21st-century response to the imaginative scope of Shakespeare's original, in which mortals and fairies collide in a moonlit forest and boundaries between the real and the imagined are blurred' (Hemming, 2021). However, perhaps the most powerful in this production were the instances in which the physical and the virtual spaces did not necessarily overlap but instead were set side by side to create the effects of doubling (Hemming, 2021).

In those moments of doubling, the production came particularly close to the viewing experience of live theatre (without attempting to replace it), in that it allowed the audience to see the fictional action as well as the actual stage and the auditorium. *Dream* also echoed a live-theatre experience by foregrounding the thrill of real-time action. Watching the actors animating the avatars, the experiencers could feel the excitement of an event unfolding in front of them in the present, while being intensely aware of the possibility of failure – on the part of the actors, as well as on the part of technology. It is through this constant engagement with theatre and theatricality that *Dream* came the closest to its source. The metatheatrical framework that it borrowed from *A Midsummer Night's Dream* was fundamental for the dramaturgy of this production as an extended reality performance, although the RSC production used Shakespeare's plots, characters, and lines very selectively.

The weakness of this adaptation, however, did not necessarily lie in its discerning approach to the source; rather, it lay in its problematic combination of media conventions and users' expectations. When applying Unreal Engine again, the RSC decided to go further and allow the paying participants to experience moments of video-game interactivity. Unfortunately, the experience of launching the fireflies and planting the seeds did not provide the users with a sense of agency, given that as part of a large audience they could not make their actions clearly discernible from the actions of others or particularly impactful in terms of *Dream*'s development. What this suggests is that while extended reality performances are likely to combine the technologies and conventions from different media, such as theatre, gaming, and cinema, it is important that users have a sound understanding of the functions of the tools and their own position as participants.

Conclusion

Several insights about the current state of the field emerge from the discussion of extended reality Shakespeare performances in this section. First, as adaptations, most works exemplify a liberal approach to their source, which might consist in radically simplifying the plot, reducing the number of characters, and condensing the text to a selection of scenes or lines. As Wolf noted about the RSC *Dream*, 'purists may well wonder what has happened to the play along the way' (Wolf, 2022), and his remark might be applied to several examples across all three categories, in particular *Current, Rising*. Such an approach prompts the question of whether it is appropriate to describe these works as Shakespeare adaptations, or whether they are too far removed from the source to qualify for this label. More importantly, one might query the artists' motivation and justification for using Shakespeare's plays. Again, in the context of *Dream*, Soloski (2021) protested that 'Shakespeare is the pretext, not the point', yet what I have sought to show in this section is that in most of these examples Shakespeare's dramas have indeed provided the creative teams with ideas on how to apply technology purposefully and creatively.

Second, the works in this section share crucial characteristics concerning their production processes, financing models, and scale. All of them required substantial team effort – they were intensely interdisciplinary and they brought together a range of companies and organisations. As such, they demonstrated how the boundary between academic and artistic projects is becoming increasingly blurred, particularly in the field of extended reality (Rauschnabel et al., 2022: 14), where rapid development of technology calls for interdisciplinary collaboration, while the high cost of design requires multi-source financing. Consequently, the makers need to pull resources from different sectors to ensure the work's creative success and financial viability. Indeed, most of the productions discussed here were created as part of research and development in collaboration with university partners, with the application of the practice-as-research model in which research is carried out through practical work. The majority of them relied on public funding for the arts, research, and innovation available in metropolitan centres in the Global North. As many as three of them (*Current,*

Rising; *Dream*; and Nexus's *Tempest*) were supported by the UK Audiences of the Future grants, even though their respective budgets varied widely. Despite different scales of financing, most performances were rather short (between ten and sixty minutes), given the cost and the complexity of designing the work but also the level of attention required from the audience to experience extended reality. Moreover, considering the cost of visual displays and headsets as well as the issues with data transfer and troubleshooting, the number of participating experiencers was often limited.

The previous two points bring me to the third common aspect of the discussed productions. Most of them were conceived as prototypes, which were developed to test digital tools in performance and advance the process of digital theatre-making. Shakespeare's plays were used each time as inspirations for understanding the potential of extended reality for experiencers. This explains why it often might have felt that the treatment of the source was instrumental and that the application of technology was underwhelming – the performances were designed as experiments with dramaturgies and devices. They were meant to trial novel approaches to performance design and take risks. Ellis articulately explained this in relation to *Dream*: 'It's not being put out as a solution, but as exploration', adding that '[t]he purpose of the project is to really push innovation, to push the technologies as far as we can' (cited in Hemming, 2021). *Dream* is a particularly relevant example here since the public discussion about this production explicitly focused on its prototype status. Writing about the 'potential' of the project, Kirwan noted how this was 'a diverting experiment', 'still in the proof-of-concept stage', and 'a demo for something that might one day be a really thrilling combination of live performance and digital artistry' (Kirwan, 2021). Similarly, O'Connell emphasised the notion of 'potential', pointing to the need for greater, Hollywood-level investment to fully realise the possibilities of virtual reality (O'Connell, 2021).

While funding is of course crucial – particularly in extended reality performances, which require high levels of expertise, advanced software and hardware, but also cross-sectional partnerships and long-term interdisciplinary collaboration – aiming for bigger budgets is not necessarily the answer. The development of extended reality performances does not depend exclusively on increasing the resources, as at the moment we still need to understand better how to design the work creatively and accessibly. The following section addresses some of the key challenges and expectations surrounding augmented and virtual reality in performance to explore the future of extended reality Shakespeare.

3 What's the Future?

In the last decade we have seen the rapid rise of augmented and virtual reality Shakespeare adaptations, discussed with some detail in Section 2, so it is natural to consider the future of extended reality in Shakespeare performance and theatre more broadly. In this final section, I offer brief conclusions about the potential of augmented and virtual reality for creating new forms of presence, embodiment, eventfulness, and interaction in performance. At the same time, I outline the technological, dramaturgical, and institutional challenges faced by makers, users, and cultural programmers. Awareness of these challenges is necessary if we want to ensure an exciting and equitable future of augmented and virtual reality in performance.

The potential of extended reality for theatre depends on the theatre's ability to reinvent itself within a novel framework of reality as an overarching and hybrid entity that combines physical and virtual realities. The notion of the hybrid is crucial here. Lavender argues that the phenomenon 'provides an increasingly pervasive mode for cultural engagement' (Lavender, 2016: 59) and defines it as 'the creation of something new from elements that are unalike' (Lavender, 2016: 63). This can result in various kinds of combination that might roughly be divided into two approaches: blending and juxtaposition. In the first case the distinctions between elements are likely to become blurred to some extent, whereas in the second they are likely to become highlighted. This confirms Izabella Pluta's observation that 'the effect of hybridisation mines the characteristics of different systems and places them in new configurations, either fused or remaining in tension' (Pluta, 2010: 187). The Shakespeare adaptations explored here oscillate between these two configurations in that they integrate augmented and virtual reality into physical spaces for the effects of both complementation and contrast. As I have argued throughout this Element, the latter scenario is particularly important as it is precisely through the effects of contrast that extended reality can heighten the experiencers' perceptions of presence and allow them to reconsider their sense of embodiment and proprioception.

The ability to bring together disparate parts makes hybrids unique, intensely present, and refreshingly disorienting. Lavender explains that a hybrid 'exists *differently*, across a boundary, in a new configuration', being 'simply *beyond* that from which it derives', and that it 'appears to us in its here and now' (Lavender, 2016: 63). This might be because, according to Marshall McLuhan, the process of combining different elements 'offers an especially favorable opportunity to notice their structural components and properties' (McLuhan, 1964 [2001]: 49). It also gives the experiencers a chance to extend and transform their perceptions of their own bodies and the bodies of others. As McLuhan notes, '[t]he moment of the meeting of media is a moment of freedom and release from the ordinary trance and numbness imposed by them on our senses' (McLuhan, 1964 [2001]: 61). Similarly, Jürgen E. Müller claims that '[m]edia-related hybrids ... set energies free which liberate our perception from habitualized patterns' (Müller, 2010: 25). It is in this sense that extended reality theatre, as a hybrid of different realities, has the potential to affect the sensorium and lead to new forms of presence and embodiment.

At the same time, what distinguishes extended reality theatre from experiences in other media and sectors that incorporate augmented and virtual reality is the emphasis on a unique event. It unfolds in real time, and even when the performers and the experiencers do not share the same physical space, they can still have the perception of being together. This perception is owing to their ability to interact in a distinctly theatrical manner and to participate in the feedback loop, which Fischer-Lichte (2008: 38) describes as fundamental to the development of performance. In the RSC *Dream*, the audiences watched the show remotely, but, because of the production's real-time dimension and the possibility of interaction with the avatars in the virtual world and the actors in the studio, they could have the sense of togetherness, even if the set-up for the interaction was imperfect and limited. Extended reality theatre can thus adapt the categories of eventfulness and social interactivity for the demands and opportunities of augmented and virtual reality. As such, it can redefine the characteristics of theatre as a live medium that relies on co-presence and co-feeling.

The development of extended reality theatre, however, still needs to overcome a series of technological, dramaturgical, and institutional challenges. If extended reality performances are to occur in real time, this makes their design both laborious and costly. It also introduces significant risk in terms of the work's delivery. As Blair MacIntyre et al. note, '*Working in real-time is difficult*. When many things are happening in a split second, and when interactions are based on possibly noisy sensor data, debugging and understanding an experience can be difficult or impossible' (MacIntyre et al., 2004: 199, italics in original). Although their observation is now almost two decades old, it is still valid given that designing extended reality performances requires access to sophisticated software, hardware, and skill sets.

The technological challenges are intrinsically linked with the dramaturgical ones. Theatre-makers and technicians work in tandem trying to answer complex questions about the integration of augmented and virtual reality in performance. What new realities are we introducing and how are they to be connected? Why do we need augmented and virtual realities to create the performance and how can we efficiently incorporate them? How do we want the participants to access the work and what instruction, guidance, and support do we need to offer them throughout the experience?

The questions around access are fundamental to the development of extended reality from the perspective of makers, experiencers, and cultural programmers. They also indicate the third challenge, which is about opening up this kind of practice to a wider group of artists and audiences. This means not only making the technology easy to use and finding the right dramaturgical solutions to involve the experiencers but also making institutional changes that allow for greater knowledge sharing and consistent funding for research and development projects.

Finally, I argue that while sleek computer graphics are undoubtedly appealing to audiences and the possibility of game-like interactivity is attractive, the future of extended reality performance lies not so much in competing with cinema and gaming industries as in establishing its own identity and modus operandi. This might consist in moving away from perfect immersion to self-reflexive combinations of realities. In charting CREW's artistic development, Joris (cited in Nedelkopoulou et al., 2014: 249) points to the company's growing interest in transitions between physical and virtual elements:

> Continuous and total absorption was possible, and that was very interesting at the beginning. We called this 'radical confluence', but soon we found that the doubt of being in the middle of two realities is far more fascinating. We decided to follow a slightly different artistic path. We'd rather have our playing field in the middle of two realities, one leg in the virtual, one leg in the real and the capacity of the mind of the immersant to balance and shift in between these two realities; what we identify as 'the transitional zone'.

The idea of 'the transitional zone' is particularly applicable to CREW's work, but it is also fundamental for our understanding of how augmented and virtual reality might function successfully in performances of Shakespeare's plays. Most of the adaptations mentioned in this Element have involved powerful transitional moments in which the seams between the physical and the virtual spaces became suddenly visible. These were the moments of heightened presence and proprioception for the experiencers, but also the moments of reflection on the nature of truth and illusion. These moments seem to have been directly inspired by Shakespeare's own insights into theatre and metatheatre and by his spirit of play and playfulness. The frequent use of Shakespeare's dramas in performances with augmented and virtual reality shows that contemporary theatre-makers continue to turn to the Renaissance playwright as they are trying to advance the development of extended reality theatre as a medium.

References

Abel, Lionel. (1963). *Metatheatre: A New View of Dramatic Form.* New York: Hill and Wang.

Aebischer, Pascale. (2020). *Shakespeare, Spectatorship and the Technologies of Performance.* Cambridge: Cambridge University Press. https://doi .org/10.1017/9781108339001.

Aebischer, Pascale. (2021). *Viral Shakespeare: Performance in the Time of Pandemic.* Cambridge: Cambridge University Press. https://doi.org/ 10.1017/9781108943482.

Allred, Gemma Kate, Benjamin Broadribb, and Erin Sullivan, eds. (2022). *Lockdown Shakespeare: New Evolutions in Performance and Adaptation.* The Arden Shakespeare. London: Bloomsbury. https://doi.org/ 10.5040/9781350247833.

Anonymous. (2021). 'Current, Rising – Royal Opera House, London (LAST CHANCE TO SEE)'. *Salterton Arts Review. London Arts, Theatre and Heritage Reviews and Recommendations.* 6 June. https://bit .ly/3tXqCt4.

Barba, Evan, Blair MacIntyre, and Elizabeth D. Mynatt. (2012). 'Here We Are! Where Are We? Locating Mixed Reality in the Age of the Smartphone'. *Proceedings of the IEEE*, 100(4): 929–36.

Bay-Cheng, Sarah. (2015). 'Taxonomy of Distortion. Along the Media Performance Continuum'. In *Performance and Media: Taxonomies for a Changing Field*, edited by Sarah Bay-Cheng, Jennifer Parker Starbuck, and David Z. Saltz, 39–64. Ann Arbor: University of Michigan Press. https://doi.org/10.3998/mpub.5582757.

Bay-Cheng, Sarah, Jennifer Parker-Starbuck, and David Z. Saltz. (2015). *Performance and Media: Taxonomies for a Changing Field.* Ann Arbor: University of Michigan Press. https://doi.org/10.3998/mpub.5582757.

Benford, Steve, and Gabriella Giannachi. (2011). *Performing Mixed Reality*. Cambridge, MA: MIT Press.

Benford, Steve, Andy Crabtree, Martin Flintham, et al. (2006). 'Can You See Me Now?'. *ACM Transactions on Computer–Human Interaction*, 13(1): 100–33. https://doi.org/10.1145/1143518.1143522.

Bolter, Jay David, and Richard Grusin. (2000). *Remediation: Understanding New Media*. Cambridge, MA: MIT Press.

Bowers, Fredson. (1940). *Elizabethan Revenge Tragedy 1587–1642*. Princeton, NJ: Princeton University Press.

Broadribb, Benjamin. (2021). 'Review of Pippa Hill's Dream (Directed by Robin McNicholas for the Royal Shakespeare Company) at Portsmouth Guildhall. Performed and Streamed Online, 12–20 March 2021'. *Shakespeare*, 17(4): 492–5. https://doi.org/10.1080/17450918.2021.1950204.

Broude, Ronald. (1975). 'Revenge and Revenge Tragedy in Renaissance England'. *Renaissance Quarterly*, 28(1): 38–58. https://doi.org/10.2307/2860421.

Bushnell, Rebecca W., and Michael Ullyot. (2022). 'Shakespeare and Virtual Reality'. In *The Routledge Handbook of Shakespeare and Interface*, edited by Clifford Werier and Paul Budra, 29–43. New York: Routledge. https://doi.org/10.4324/9780367821722-4.

Cartelli, Thomas. (2019). *Reenacting Shakespeare in the Shakespeare Aftermath: The Intermedial Turn and Turn to Embodiment*. New York: Palgrave Macmillan. https://doi.org/10.1057/978-1-137-40482-4.

Causey, Matthew. (2016). 'Postdigital Performance'. *Theatre Journal*, 68(3): 427–41. https://doi.org/10.1353/tj.2016.0074.

Clapp, Susannah. (2021). 'Dream Review – The RSC's Hi-tech Shakespeare Only Goes So Far'. *Guardian*. 21 March. https://bit.ly/3u3fyuF.

Coghlan, Alexandra. (2021). 'Current, Rising, Royal Opera House Review – A Joyful Celebration of Storytelling Possibility'. *Arts Desk*. 21 May. https://bit.ly/49D3G2X.

Çöltekin, Arzu, Ian Lochhead, Marguerite Madden, et al. (2020). 'Extended Reality in Spatial Sciences: A Review of Research Challenges and Future Directions'. *ISPRS International Journal of Geo-Information*, 9(439): 1–29. https://doi.org/10.3390/ijgi9070439.

Crouch, Tim. (2022). *Truth's a Dog Must to Kennel*. London: Methuen Drama.

Dalton, Jeremy. (2021). *Reality Check: How Immersive Technologies Can Transform Your Business*. London: Kogan Page.

Embley, Jochan. (2021). 'Current, Rising at the Royal Opera House Review: A Terrifically Trippy Opera Experience'. *Evening Standard*. 19 May. https://bit.ly/3FPuoaA.

Falk, Dan. (2014). *The Science of Shakespeare: A New Look at the Playwright's Universe*. New York: Thomas Dunne Books.

Fischer-Lichte, Erika. (2008). *The Transformative Power of Performance: A New Aesthetics*. Translated by Saskya Iris Jain. London: Routledge.

Furht, Borko, ed. (2011). *Handbook of Augmented Reality*. New York: Springer. https://doi.org/10.1007/978-1-4614-0064-6.

Georgi, Claudia. (2014) *Liveness on Stage: Intermedial Challenges in Contemporary British Theatre and Performance*. Berlin: Walter de Gruyter.

Goode, Lauren. (2019). 'Get Ready to Hear a Lot More About "XR"'. *Wired*. 5 January. www.wired.com/story/what-is-xr/.

Hall, George. (2021). 'Current, Rising'. *Stage*. 20 May. www.thestage.co.uk/reviews/current-rising.

Hemming, Sarah. (2021). 'Poetry and Motion Capture in a High-Tech *Dream*'. *Financial Times*. 12 March. www.ft.com/content/805f3431-cbd0-4186-b5d4-cc3fd94617e7.

Hewett, Ivan. (2021). 'Current, Rising, Royal Opera House, Review: "Virtual Reality" Is No Match for Serious Opera'. *The Telegraph*. 21 May. https://bit.ly/47l6uj7.

Holz, Thomas, Abraham G. Campbell, Gregory M. P. O'Hare, John W. Stafford, Alan Martin, and Mauro Dragone. (2011). 'MiRA – Mixed Reality Agents'. *International Journal of Human–Computer Studies*, 69(4): 251–68. https://doi:10.1016/j.ijhcs.2010.10.001.

Jenkins, Henry. (2006). *Convergence Culture: Where Old and New Media Collide*. New York: New York University Press.

Kattenbelt, Chiel. (2006). 'Theatre as the Art of the Performer and the Stage of Intermediality'. In *Intermediality in Theatre and Performance*, edited by Freda Chapple and Chiel Kattenbelt, 29–39. Amsterdam: Rodopi. https://doi.org/10.1163/9789401210089.

Kattenbelt, Chiel. (2008). 'Intermediality in Theatre and Performance: Definitions, Perceptions and Medial Relationships'. *Cultura, Lenguaje y Representación [Culture, Language & Representation]*, 6 (La Intermedialidad [Intermediality]): 19–29.

Kattenbelt, Chiel. (2010). 'Intermediality in Performance and as a Mode of Performativity'. In *Mapping Intermediality in Performance*, edited by Sarah Bay-Cheng, Chiel Kattenbelt, Andy Lavender, and Robin Nelson, 29–37. Amsterdam: Amsterdam University Press. https://doi.org/10.5117/9789089642554.

Kattenbelt, Chiel. (2021). 'On Artistic Research, Intermediality and the "Hamlet Encounters" Project'. In *Performing/Transforming: Transgressions and Hybridizations Across Texts, Media, Bodies*, edited by Floriana Puglisi, 17–37. Torino: Otto.

Kaye, Nick. (2000). *Site-Specific Art: Performance, Place and Documentation*. London: Routledge.

Kirwan, Peter. (2021). 'Dream Online (Royal Shakespeare Company) @ online'. University of Nottingham Blog Post. 20 March. https://bit.ly/3FNER6x.

Kott, Jan. (1967). *Shakespeare Our Contemporary*. Translated by Bolesław Taborski. London: Methuen.

Lamb, Hilary. (2021). 'Theatre Review: "Dream", the Royal Shakespeare Company'. *Engineering and Technology*. 17 March. https://bit.ly/3Qr5zqy.

Lavender, Andy. (2016). *Performance in the Twenty-First Century: Theatres of Engagement*. London: Routledge. https://doi.org/10.4324/9780203128176.

Lewis, C. S. (1964). *Discarded Image: An Introduction to Medieval and Renaissance Literature*. Cambridge: Cambridge University Press.

Li Lan, Yong. (2003). 'Shakespeare as Virtual Event'. *Theatre Research International*, 28(1): 46–60. https://doi.org/10.1017/S0307883303000142.

MacIntyre, Blair, Maribeth Gandy, Steven Dow, and Jay David Bolter. (2004). 'DART: A Toolkit for Rapid Design Exploration of Augmented Reality Experiences'. In *Proceedings of the 17th Annual ACM Symposium on User Interface Software and Technology (UIST '04)*. ACM, New York, 197–206. https://doi.org/10.1145/1029632.1029669.

Mancewicz, Aneta. (2014). *Intermedial Shakespeares on European Stages*. Basingstoke: Palgrave Macmillan. https://doi.org/10.1057/9781137360045.

Mancewicz, Aneta. (2018). 'From Global London to Global Shakespeare'. *Contemporary Theatre Review*, 28(2): 235–46. https://doi.org/10.1080/10486801.2017.1365716.

Mancewicz, Aneta. (2023). 'Liveness in VR and AR Shakespeare Adaptations'. In *Early Modern Liveness: Mediating Presence in Text, Stage and Screen*, edited by Danielle Rosvally and Donovan Sherman, 89–110. The Arden Shakespeare. London: Bloomsbury. https://doi.org/10.5040/9781350318502.0012.

McLuhan, Marshall. (1964 [2001]). *Understanding Media: The Extensions of Man*. London: Routledge.

Milgram, Paul, and Fumio Kishino. (1994). 'A Taxonomy of Mixed Reality Visual Displays'. *IEICE Transactions on Information Systems*, E77-D(12): 1321–9.

Milgram, Paul, Haruo Takemura, Akira Utsumi, and Fumio Kishino. (1994). 'Augmented Reality: A Class of Displays on the Reality–Virtuality Continuum'. *Proceedings of SPIE – The International Society for Optical Engineering*, 2351, Telemanipulator and Telepresence Technologies: 282–92. https://doi.org/10.1117/12.197321.

Müller, Jürgen E. (2010). 'Intermediality and Media Historiography in the Digital Era'. *Acta Universitatis Sapientiae, Film, and Media Studies*, 2: 15–38.

Nedelkopoulou, Eirini, Eric Joris, Philippe Bekaert, and Kurt Vanhoutte. (2014). 'On the Border Between Performance, Science and the Digital: A Conversation with CREW'. *International Journal of Performance Arts and Digital Media*, 10(2): 246–54. https://doi.org/10.1080/14794713.2014.946290.

Nelson, Robin. (2010). 'Experiencer'. In *Mapping Intermediality in Performance*, edited by Sarah Bay-Cheng, Chiel Kattenbelt, Andy Lavender, and Robin Nelson, 45. Amsterdam: Amsterdam University Press. https://doi.org/10.5117/9789089642554.

Nelson, Robin. (2022). *Practice as Research in the Arts (and Beyond): Principles, Processes, Contexts, Achievements*, 2nd ed. Cham: Palgrave Macmillan. https://doi.org/10.1007/978-3-030-90542-2.

O'Connell, Jarlath. (2021). 'RSC's Dream Online'. *The American*. 17 March. www.theamerican.co.uk/pr/rev-th-RSC-Dream-Online.

Oliver, Ben. (2020). 'The Royal Opera House Presents *Current, Rising*, the World's First Opera in Hyper Reality'. Royal Opera House News. 23 November. https://bit.ly/3SQR7uX.

Ormerod, Peter. (2021). 'REVIEW: RSC's Experimental Dream Gives an Intriguing Glimpse into the Future of Live Entertainment'. *Northampton Chronicle & Echo*. 17 March. https://bit.ly/3MBWXfo.

Penn, Louise. (2021). 'Review: Dream (RSC, VR Online)'. 21 March. https://loureviews.blog/2021/03/21/review-dream-rsc-vr-online/.

Pluta, Izabella. (2010). 'Hybridity'. In *Mapping Intermediality in Performance*, edited by Sarah Bay-Cheng, Chiel Kattenbelt, Andy Lavender, and Robin Nelson, 186–7. Amsterdam: Amsterdam University Press. https://doi.org/10.5117/9789089642554.

Postlewait, Thomas, and Tracy C. Davis. (2003). 'Theatricality: An Introduction'. In *Theatricality*, edited by Tracy C. Davis and Thomas Postlewait, 1–39. Cambridge: Cambridge University Press.

Punathambekar, Aswin, and Sriram Mohan. (2019). 'Introduction: Mapping Global Digital Cultures'. In *Global Digital Cultures: Perspectives from South Asia*, edited by Aswin Punathambekar and Sriram Mohan. Ann Arbor: University of Michigan Press. https://doi.org/10.3998/mpub.9561751.

Rauschnabel, Philipp A., Reto Felix, Chris Hinsch, Hamza Shahab, and Florian Alt. (2022). 'What Is XR? Towards a Framework for Augmented and Virtual Reality'. *Computers in Human Behavior* 133, article 107289: 1–18. https://doi.org/10.1016/j.chb.2022.107289.

Roberts-Smith, Jennifer. (2022). 'What Can Shakespeare Do for Virtual Reality?'. In *Shakespeare and Virtual Reality*, edited by Stephen Wittek and David McInnis, 4–11. Cambridge: Cambridge University Press. https://doi.org/10.1017/9781009003995.

Robinett, Warren. (1992). 'Synthetic Experience: A Proposed Taxonomy'. *Presence*, 1(2): 229–47. https://doi.org/10.1162/pres.1992.1.2.229.

Rouse, Rebecca. (2015). 'MR^x as a Performative and Theatrical Stage'. *Digital Creativity*, 26(3–4): 193–206. https://doi.org/10.1080/14626268.2015.1100121.

Rouse, Rebecca, Maria Engberg, Nassim JafariNaimi, and Jay David Bolter. (2015). 'MR^x: An Interdisciplinary Framework for Mixed Reality Experience Design and Criticism'. *Digital Creativity*, 26(3–4): 175–81. https://doi.org/10.1080/14626268.2015.1100123.

RSC. (2021a). 'Dream Q&A'. https://bit.ly/3u83ath.

RSC. (2021b). 'In Conversation with Pippa Hill and Robin McNicholas'. https://bit.ly/3u5pELw.

Sauter, Willmar. (2000). *The Theatrical Event: Dynamics of Performance and Perception*. Iowa City: University of Iowa Press.

Schmitt, Carl. (2006). *Hamlet or Hecuba: The Irruption of Time into Play*. Translated by Simona Draghici. Corvallis, OR: Plutarch Press.

Sen, Amrita, ed. (2022). 'Introduction: Experiencing Digital Shakespeares in the Global South'. In *Digital Shakespeares from the Global South*, edited by Amrita Sen. Cham: Palgrave Macmillan. https://doi.org/10.1007/978-3-031-04787-9.

Shakespeare, William. (1999). *The Tempest*. Edited by Virginia Mason Vaughan and Alden T. Vaughan. The Arden Shakespeare. London: Thomson Learning.

Shakespeare, William. (2007). *Hamlet*. Edited by Ann Thompson and Neil Taylor. The Arden Shakespeare. London: Thomson Learning.

Shakespeare, William. (2017). *A Midsummer Night's Dream*. Edited by Sukanta Chaudhuri. The Arden Shakespeare. London: Bloomsbury.

Soloski, Alexis. (2021). 'Review: Living the "Dream," on Your Laptop or Phone.' *New York Times*. 17 March. https://bit.ly/47546NK.

Speicher, Maximilian, Brian D. Hall, and Michael Nebeling. (2019). 'What Is Mixed Reality?'. In *CHI Conference on Human Factors in Computing Systems Proceedings (CHI 2019)*, 4–9 May, Glasgow, Scotland, UK, ACM, New York, USA. https://doi.org/10.1145/3290605.

Sullivan, Erin. (2022). *Shakespeare and Digital Performance in Practice*. Cham: Palgrave Macmillan. https://doi.org/10.1007/978-3-031-05763-2.

Sutherland, Gill. (2021). 'Interview: EM Williams on Playing Puck in New Digital Dream Now on at the RSC'. *Stratford-upon-Avon Herald*. 13 March. https://bit.ly/3sxqAaX.

Vanhoutte, Kurt, and Charlotte Bigg. (2014). 'On the Border Between Performance, Science and the Digital: The Embodied Orrery'.

International Journal of Performance Arts and Digital Media, 10(2): 255–60. https://doi.org/10.1080/14794713.2014.946291.

Webber, Samuel. (2004). *Theatricality as Medium*. New York: Fordham University Press. https://doi.org/10.5422/fso/9780823224159.003.0001.

Weijdom, Joris. (2017). *Mixed Reality and the Theatre of the Future: Fresh Perspectives on Arts and New Technologies*. Brussels: IETM. www.ietm.org.

Wittek, Stephen, and David McInnis. (2022). *Shakespeare and Virtual Reality*. Cambridge: Cambridge University Press. https://doi.org/10.1017/9781009003995.

Wolf, Matt. (2022). 'RSC "Dream" Is an Inventive, Condensed Take on the Bard'. *London Theatre*. 25 January. https://bit.ly/3QQcb37.

Worthen, W. B. (2017). 'Shakespearean Technicities'. In *The Oxford Handbook of Shakespeare and Performance*, edited by James C. Bulman, 321–40. Oxford: Oxford University Press. https://doi.org/10.1093/oxfordhb/9780199687169.013.36.

Worthen, W. B. (2020). *Shakespeare, Technicity, Theatre*. Cambridge: Cambridge University Press. https://doi.org/10.1017/9781108628464.

Wynants, Nele, Kurt Vanhoutte, and Philippe Bekaert. (2008). 'Being Inside the Image – Heightening the Sense of Presence in a Video Captured Environment through Artistic Means: The Case of CREW'. In *PRESENCE 2008, Proceedings of the 11th Annual International Workshop on Presence*. Padova, 16–18 October. Edited by Anna Spagnolli and Luciano Gamberini, 157–62. Padova: CLEUP.

Acknowledgements

I want to thank Bill Worthen for intellectual inspiration and his support as Series Editor. My understanding of extended reality owes greatly to my collaborators Eric Joris, Chiel Kattenbelt, and Robin Nelson, with whom I have worked on Shakespeare and technology for more than a decade. I truly appreciate their intuitions, ideas, and friendship. The Element has benefitted from their invaluable feedback. I extend my gratitude to anonymous reviewers who offered helpful insights and recommendations. I am also grateful to Rebecca Bushnell and Amrita Sen for sharing their exciting work in progress. Images and videos in this Element are reproduced with the kind permission of Colin Davis and Valentina Tarelli (Nexus Studios), Eric Joris (CREW), Joanna Scotcher, the Royal Shakespeare Company, Manchester International Festival, Marshmallow Laser Feast, and Philharmonia Orchestra. Finally, I am thankful to Salvatore Florio for encouragement and advice. This Element is dedicated to him.

Cambridge Elements ☰

Shakespeare Performance

W. B. Worthen
Barnard College

W. B. Worthen is Alice Brady Pels Professor in the Arts, and
Chair of the Theatre Department at Barnard College. He is also
co-chair of the Ph.D. Program in Theatre at Columbia University,
where he is Professor of English and Comparative Literature.

ABOUT THE SERIES

Shakespeare Performance is a dynamic collection in a field that is both always emerging and always evanescent. Responding to the global range of Shakespeare performance today, the series launches provocative, urgent criticism for researchers, graduate students and practitioners. Publishing scholarship with a direct bearing on the contemporary contexts of Shakespeare performance, it considers specific performances, material and social practices, ideological and cultural frameworks, emerging and significant artists and performance histories.

Cambridge Elements ≡

Shakespeare Performance

Printed in the United States
by Baker & Taylor Publisher Services